THE EARLY COUNTY MASSACRE

GOOLSBY VS. THE STATE OF GEORGIA

ORICE JENKINS

THE
History
PRESS

Published by The History Press
Charleston, SC
www.historypress.com

Unless otherwise noted, images are from the author's collection.

First published 2024

Manufactured in the United States

ISBN 9781467156936

Library of Congress Control Number: 2023950630

Notice: The information in this book is true and complete to the best of our knowledge. It is offered without guarantee on the part of the author or The History Press. The author and The History Press disclaim all liability in connection with the use of this book.

In memory of the Goolsbys:
Grandison, Mary, Ulysses, Mike, Roosevelt and Nathaniel.

In memory of the innocent victims and survivors of the Early County Race
Massacre: Simon Goolsby, Early Hightower, Edmond Law, Precious Hall,
George Winget Harris, Martin "Hash" Jewell, Edward Jewell,
Charlie Holmes, Julian Goolsby, Charlotte Henderson, Charlie Givens,
Isom Crews, Beulah Crews, Fredonia Harris, Martha Mozee, Laura Bush,
Rena Law, Gus Stringer and countless others.

CONTENTS

FOREWORD

A Letter to My Ancestors:

To the Great Elders who came before me, I greet you with deep gratitude. I've come to understand that the timing of life's events is always divine, and within each experience, there is a profound lesson to be learned. Your enduring presence in my life has been a source of strength and guidance, and I now recognize that I've felt your watchful eyes upon me throughout my journey. We share some of the same gifts, talents and skills, and it's an honor, a pleasure and a privilege to discover my roots, to understand where I come from and to embrace the essence of who I am because of you.

I must admit that in my younger days, I harbored some resentment toward my last name, as it often became fodder for childhood teasing. However, I've come to realize that it was you who bestowed on me the angelic presence of my father. He not only comforted me but also instilled in me the profound strength and significance of my name. Today, I wear Goolsby like a badge of honor, akin to it being emblazoned on a warrior's chest.

My heart brims with gratitude as I embark on this full-circle journey with my father. Witnessing the skills we share in artistry and craftsmanship, I've come to understand that these abilities trace back to our ancestors, who were master craftsmen, builders, farmers and preachers. The compassionate heart that beats within me and my father's unwavering dedication to serving others are threads woven into the very fabric of our family lineage. How could one not be immensely proud of such a heritage?

I'm acutely aware of the privilege I hold in making this connection, for so many of my African American brothers and sisters may never have the same opportunity, robbed as they are of this link to their past. I cherish your presence in my life, for it has fortified me to face the challenges of being a Black person in the United States with courage and resilience. Thank you for guiding me through life's tribulations and for the silent yet steadfast Goolsby temperament that runs in my veins. I implore your continued invisible guidance and support as I embark on this ongoing journey, vowing to regularly commune with you in gratitude.

I extend my heartfelt appreciation to Orice for his labor of love in creating this book, a testament to my family's enduring legacy. As I enter the elder season of my life, bearing witness to my parents as they approach their homecoming, I'm acutely aware that our time together in this dimension will soon end. However, their spirits, like yours, will remain ever-present. Just as the energy of those who came before me continues to resonate within me, so too will the love and wisdom of my ancestors remain a guiding force in my life.

With pride and reverence,

Shar

To Those Who Don't Know Me:

I am Shar Goolsby, and I assert my right to exist. My very existence is a divinely orchestrated miracle. This story delves into one of the generational wounds I am duty-bound to heal. For most of my life, I grappled with a sense of displacement, unsure of where I truly belonged. Growing up in Atlanta, it never felt like home. Grounding myself, finding safety and securing a sense of identity have been lifelong pursuits shaped by the lessons I believe my soul was destined to learn. The presence of my ancestors lingers with me, carrying with it their enduring pain.

The introduction to and my blossoming relationship with my cousin Orice have provided me with a profound full-circle moment. While talking with my father in his den one day about family legacy and connection, I received a notification on my phone from Orice. At this time, he was unknown to me, but his message led me to know he was not someone I had to fear. Anyone who even knew of the existence of my family's story at this point in life is definitely not a threat. That message, on what seemed to be a random Sunday afternoon, led to the unraveling of what had become a mystery and a legend. Because of Orice, I have learned who I am and where I come from and have visited the land that my great-grandparents owned.

Reconnecting with the land where my ancestors were once enslaved, where they toiled, cultivated, eventually owned and now rest in eternal peace, has granted me a sense of belonging and oneness I've never before experienced. While standing on this southern country farmland, and visiting gravesites of my family, I felt a sense of HOME and an overwhelming presence of ancestral souls. In the heart of Manhattan or the bustle of D.C., I've felt more alone than I did on that day in Blakely. It was as if my family had finally come home to the land that was their sanctuary. To my knowledge, I am the first descendant of Ulysses or Mike A. Goolsby to touch the land they once called home. Regrettably, my eighty-seven-year-old father has been unable to visit the land we now know the location of, due to the emotional trauma embedded in our family's history.

Although my father did not father any sons, his bloodline will live on through my nephew. I am committed to teaching him about the sacrifices our ancestors were forced to make. More importantly, I will empower him with the knowledge of his heritage so that he may embrace a deeper sense of self by knowing who he is and where he comes from. Most crucially, I will ensure that he understands the ever-present guidance and support of our ancestors on his journey through life.

I carry a gift of healing that has been supported by my ancestors. I am a licensed and certified healthcare provider of physiotherapy and energetic medicine. I am currently working toward licensure and certification in clinical mental health counseling with a specialization in trauma. My treatment approach integrates energetic, physical, emotional and psychological healing to strengthen the body's ability to heal itself. I serve my community as my ancestors did.

Another divine mystery is that presently, the land adjacent to the location of the original historic injustice is for sale in Early County. For those of you who are interested in honoring the memory of those who lost their lives, I invite you to visit Orice's website to donate toward the purchase of this land. The mission is to create a healing sanctuary and wellness center that provides healing support for the community and all others in need of healing generational trauma. We welcome donations to my organization, Leap of Faith Healing Sanctuary and Gardens Foundation. I have dedicated several years of my life to increasing access to wellness and would be honored to bring my work to my ancestral homeland.

PREFACE

In 2017, I visited Georgia for the first time to attend a family reunion in Albany. When I arrived, I set my sights on visiting a small town called Blakely, where my grandmother was born. One of my relatives heard that I was making a trip to Blakely, and she asked that I try to find information on one thing: "Grandison's Uprising." I had no idea what she was talking about, but she was able to elaborate in later conversations. She explained that her aunt Charlotte Reynolds married a man named Julian Ransome Goolsby and that they were schoolteachers in Early County, Georgia, when the uprising occurred. Blakely is the county seat of Early County, in southwestern Georgia.

My cousin told me that Charlotte and Julian were hiding in a schoolhouse with no way to escape from the lynching mobs. Charlotte's father, William Reynolds, came to the rescue. He drove up with a covered wagon that he used to hide Charlotte and Julian. William had a white father and a biracial mother, and because he looked white, no one stopped him during the ongoing race war. William was able to save his daughter and son-in-law from the deadly event that was in progress.

I was never able to find documentation of this part of the tragedy, but Charlotte Reynolds told it directly to the cousin who told it to me. An internet search easily showed that there was a lot of trouble surrounding the Goolsby name in 1915. In explicit terms, it was a mass lynching, in which several Black people were killed by white mobs over three days, led by the sheriff of Early County. These lynchings were unique in that several

Left: Charlotte Reynolds Henderson, the first wife of Julian Ransome Goolsby. *Family photo.*

Below: Charlotte and Julian Goolsby were married on December 23, 1913, in Early County, Georgia.

MARRIAGE LICENSE.

STATE OF GEORGIA, COUNTY OF EARLY.

To Any Judge, Justice of the Peace, or Minister of the Gospel:

YOU ARE HEREBY AUTHORIZED TO JOIN

Julian Goolsby and *Charlotte Reynolds*

in the Holy State of Matrimony, according to the Constitution and Laws of this State, and for so doing this shall be your license. And you are hereby required to return this License to me with your certificate hereon of the fact and date of the marriage.

Given under my hand and seal, this 23rd day of Dec , 191 *3*

G. D. Olin

ORDINARY. (L. S.)

STATE OF GEORGIA, COUNTY OF EARLY. CERTIFICATE

I certify that *Julian Goolsby* and *Charlotte Reynolds* were joined in Matrimony by me, this 23 day of Dec. , Nineteen Hundred and *Thirteen*

G. D. Walker M G

G D Olin , Ordinary.

Recorded , 19

---

of the victims fought back. Grandison Goolsby shot at least three of the white people who were trying to kill him. The incidents are collectively referred to as the Grandison Goolsby War, but in my opinion, Grandison is not the central figure of this story.

The first two acts of violence were committed by Henry J. Villepigue, a white man. The intended victim in both acts was Ulysses Goolsby, a Black adolescent, who would spend the rest of his young life targeted by his government. Grandison Goolsby put his life on the line to protect and defend Ulysses, his oldest son. This made it much more heartbreaking to come across an article reporting that Ulysses and his brother Mike were burned alive in a cabin during the uprising.

There are hundreds of articles listing the names of several people who were declared lynching victims during this incident. The lists contradict each other, and for a while, I didn't know what to believe. Eventually, I found proof that Ulysses and several other reported victims survived the lynching, painting a different story than what the national news portrayed. Conversely, there were slain individuals who weren't mentioned in the widespread coverage. Two lynching memorials have been erected that commemorate

William M. Reynolds, father-in-law of Julian Goolsby at the time of the massacre. *Family photo.*

this tragedy, and both have victim lists that are incorrect or incomplete. A seemingly accurate account was found in the *Early County News* archives, and the story has been partially told in several books and local plays throughout the past century.

In 2020, I discovered eyewitness written accounts from several of the story's subjects at the Early County Courthouse. No one knew these documents were there, as they had been placed there in 1916. I made copies of everything I could and read it all in my hotel room that night. I realized that there was so much more to the story than I had imagined. It was much deeper than a race war and had never been publicly told from the perspective of the victims, their immediate families and their closest friends.

With so much information at my fingertips, I knew it was up to me to put this book together. The majority of this account comes directly from the people involved, their words ascertained from legal court documents, newspapers and genealogical sources. The "cherry on top of the cake" was finding a videotaped recording of Mrs. Girlie Harrison, Grandison Goolsby's first cousin, where she explains exactly what happened from her

This page and opposite: This memorial for Georgia's lynching victims is located at the Absalom Jones Center for Racial Healing in Atlanta, Georgia.

point of view. She was seventeen years old when the "race war" started. Her account matched what I had already written, and it filled in the holes left by the other testimonies. In my opinion, the best part was that she gave a genealogy of the family, which helped me realize that Grandison's mother, Sarah, was the daughter of Edmond and Hulda Law. I had been studying slavery records of the Law family for years, but I never noticed the infant named Sarah in those documents.

EARLY HIGHTOWER
ED LAW
ELLA BARBER
EULA BARBER
GRANDISON GOOLSBY
JESSE BARBER
JOHN RIGGINS
LEO M. FRANK
PETER FAMBROUGH
PETER MORRIS
PRECIOUS LAW

I am not a blood relative to Grandison Goolsby, but I have several connections to his family. His mother's brother, Warren Law, married my ancestor Elizabeth Horn in 1873. His own brother, Simon Goolsby, was the stepfather of my uncle Clarence Bass. His wife's relative Amy Hutchins married my ancestor Albert Terrell in 1865. They were the first Black people to be legally married in Early County. In 1871, Albert was a trustee of the Pleasant Grove AME Church. This church represents another centerpiece of the story. The victims of the Early County Massacre are undoubtedly buried at Pleasant Grove in unmarked graves. Assumedly, they are near the grave of Grandison's father, Mike Goolsby, which I visited in 2022.

The Pleasant Grove community before 1916 could've been considered a rural version of Tulsa's Black Wall Street. Much of the farmland was owned by Black people, working for themselves and making money doing so. It's hard to believe that the following was printed in the *Early County News* on April 13, 1905:

> *R.F.D. No. 5 has the best colored people in Early County.... They are all good, hardworking people, a great many owning their farms. They are courteous and polite, law-abiding citizens.*

R.F.D. No. 5 was the Rural Free Delivery mail route that served the Pleasant Grove area. The article proceeded to name several Pleasant Grove community members, such as Charlie Holmes, G.R. Goolsby (Grandison) and Early Hightower—all of whom were attacked by a lynching mob just ten years after this editorial was printed. It goes to show how quickly things can change for an entire population. The people of Pleasant Grove and their contributions should never be forgotten.

Less than three years before that article, Grandison was mentioned individually in a similar regard. The newspaper publisher commonly recognized people who stopped by his office during the week. When

Left: The grave of Mike Goolsby, Grandison Goolsby's father.

Opposite: The current cornerstone of Pleasant Grove Church in Early County, Georgia.

Grandison stopped by, the editor noted that "if all his race were like Goolsby there would be no race problem to discuss." This stems from the absurd and prevailing belief that Black people are to blame for racial issues in America. The notion is shattered by the fate of Grandison Goolsby, Blakely's model citizen, yet there was no retraction printed. This hypocrisy has remained unchallenged for several decades.

Even with all the death and destruction that occurred during the massacre, this is not a story of defeat. This is a story of survival and perseverance. This is a story of fighting back against oppressive action. These people watched the senseless murders of their family members and still found a way to keep going. Many left the South, moving to places such as Cleveland, Ohio, and Pittsburgh, Pennsylvania, where they raised their families without fear of being lynched. Some stayed in the South but moved to more progressive places such as Atlanta, Georgia, or Jacksonville, Florida. Others stayed right in Early County, where they were constantly reminded of the horrors they had lived through. That didn't stop them from living out their lives and trying to rebuild what was lost. Early County is still a beautiful place, but one can only imagine what it would've been like if this act of terror never occurred.

Charlotte and Julian Goolsby survived many more years after the massacre, but their marriage did not. Charlotte migrated to Hartford,

R. F. D. No. 5 has the best colored people in Early county, and this is another thing that we are proud of. They don't have any before-day clubs. They don't have any of these night suppers, beat and kill one another. Instead of that kind of living, they are all good, hard working people, a great many owning their own farms. They are courteous and polite, law-abiding citizens. The records of the courts of Early county will bear me out in this assertion. There is no section of this county where there has been as little court scrapes among the colored people as there is among those of R. F. D. No. 5. And we are not ashamed to give you a few of their names, which we will do : Seab Perry, John Ridley, Perry Hayes, Dan Pruitt, Ed McIntosh, Walter Glenn, Charlie Holmes, Dave Hollinger, Neal Jenkins, Joe Jenkins, Turner Jenkins, G. H. Hutchins, Charlie Cowart, Wm. Murphy, Plowden Lewis, Mike Goolsby, G. R. Goolsby, R. W. Goolsby, Early Hightower, Rev. N. Singleton, Yancy Cowart, O. M. Hutchins, Sip Haugabook, Jim C. Crew, Rev. Freeman Bryant, James F. Foster, John T. Jordan, A. L. Butler, Mack Crew, Jim Crawford, Alfred Hutchins, Jake Harris, Charles Hutchins, Morgan Hutchins, Felix Goolsby, Rance Goolsby, Peter Smith, Henry Smith, Shep Cowart, George Worrell, Idus Tull, Sam Tull, Henry Lee, Jack Wright and Henry Fields. It is impossible to mention all, but I want to say that these colored people are lifting up a high standard for their race.

DAN TUCKER.

Left: This article was written anonymously under the pseudonym "Dan Tucker." *Georgia Historic Newspapers.*

Opposite: This excerpt was printed on page five of the November 20, 1902 issue of the *Early County News. Georgia Historic Newspapers.*

G. R. Goolsby, one of our good colored farmers, who has been read ing the NEWS for ten years, dropped in last Saturday to have his date moved up to date. If all his race were like Goolsby there would be no race problem to dis- cuss.

Connecticut, my hometown, where she remarried twice and died as a widow. She outlived her children, Lura and Monzellous Goolsby, both of whom died before reaching adulthood. Julian remarried in Blakely and later migrated to Ohio, where many members of the Goolsby family ended up. Other researchers have asserted that Grandison Goolsby survived and escaped to Ohio as well. This claim is unfounded, but understandable, considering the amount of Goolsbys that left Georgia for Ohio and the inconsistencies in the newspaper articles about the lynchings.

Racial violence in 2020 caused people to recall the race massacres of the early twentieth century such as Tulsa, Elaine and Rosewood. The Early County Massacre predates all three of those. Maps were shared on social media that showed dozens of locations where these incidents occurred. Early County was not identified as one of those locations. The purpose of this book is to humanize the victims, celebrate the survivors, contextualize the events and tell the truth about the Early County Massacre—for the first time ever. This is a story that has been waiting to be told since 1915.

ACKNOWLEDGEMENTS

This book would not have been possible without the support of my family and friends, many of whom have Blakely roots: Joseph, Monica, Adonna and Shar Goolsby; Belva Foster; Brice T. Williams; Gabrielle Thomas; Gayle Anderson; Janie Thomas; Elsie R. Howard; Shebra Pitt; Shirley McDowell; Jill Jones; Bernice Bennett; Dr. Mary K. Clark; Donnie Perry; Dave Gillarm; everyone at the Georgia Archives; and Vanessa Jenkins.

1

MATRIMONY

The late December rainstorm must have seemed like an omen from its onset. Unceasingly, it descended on the rich farmland of Early County, Georgia, as Ulysses Goolsby watched, waiting for the sun to return from behind the clouds. If the weather cleared up soon, there was still time to get to the wedding reception. Celebratory events were few and far between during the warmer seasons, leaving Ulysses with a strong wintertime yearning to leave the house for something other than fieldwork. When it was too cold to work, young laborers finally had the opportunity to experience privileges such as going to school or getting married. Holidays also provided a chance for these events, so three days after Christmas was a prime time for a wedding.

Ulysses was elated when he was invited to attend the matrimonial rites of Leila Mae Smith and Major John Powell. Leila's father, Isaiah Smith, was a distant cousin of Ulysses's father, Grandison Goolsby. The ceremony took place on December 27, 1915, but Ulysses was determined to go to the "infair"—a celebration of the couple that occurred later. Major and Leila's infair was on the following day at the Oak Grove African Methodist Episcopal Church. With no access to fully covered transportation, it was not wise to travel while it was pouring out. The Goolsbys had a beautiful black buggy with red wheels and even a convertible top, but any passengers would still be exposed to the elements from the front and side. Eventually, the precipitation dissipated, and Grandison told his son that he could go ahead.

Above: Grandison and Mary Goolsby with their oldest sons, Ulysses and Mike, circa 1900. *Family photo.*

Opposite: Leila Smith Powell. *Family photo.*

It was late afternoon by the time Ulysses went outside to get his mule and buggy and started out toward Charlie Givens's house on the Howard Landing Road. It was only four miles away from the Goolsbys' house, but it might have seemed like forty miles after waiting all day. Charlie was sitting outside his house with his father, who lived in the next house. Ulysses was there to pick up Charlie Givens's little sister Lillie Bell Givens and escort her to the infair. She lived there with her brother and his wife, Willie Wiggins Givens. It started to rain again, so they all went in the house. Charlie and Lillie  Bell's younger sister Mollie was also inside, along with her wedding date, Tobe Harris.

Once the rain stopped, Ulysses, Lillie Bell, Mollie and Tobe piled into Ulysses's buggy and another buggy to head to the wedding. The Oak Grove Church was only a mile from Charlie's house, and Ulysses was sure that the rain wouldn't prevent them from finally reaching their destination. But only five hundred yards away from the church, they ran into a fate worse than downpour: an angry white man.

Henry J. Villepigue was new to Early County, hired as an overseer for Edwin Coachman's plantation on the Chattahoochee River, which separates Georgia from Alabama. He was also riding in a packed buggy and was screaming at Ulysses before their vehicles were within fifty feet of each other.

"Get out of the road!" He hollered as if the four Black juveniles were ambulatory torpedoes covered in poisonous thorns. Ulysses stopped and pulled over, but there was a clay bank at the edge of the road. He pulled his mule up on the bank and into a cotton patch, but the buggy couldn't go up there. Villepigue was not pleased and stepped out of his buggy with his pistol. His rage was compounded with an icy stare as he stomped to the back of Ulysses's buggy, pointing the gun at his head. The boys in Villepigue's buggy intervened.

"Stop, Mr. Henry!" said Lane Coachman, who probably recognized the Givens sisters.

"He's not going to kill you," warned Hassel Dumas, whose father was the presiding reverend at the Blakely Baptist Church.

Villepigue weighed his options. He was supposed to drop off Lane and Hassel in town and continue on to pick up his wife in Albany, sixty

Above: Major John Powell and Leila Smith Powell, after settling in Pennsylvania. *Family photo.*

Opposite, top: Oak Grove Church in 2023.

Opposite, bottom: Several dirt roads still exist in Early County today, with clay banks that would make it difficult to pull a buggy out of the road.

miles away. He started back toward his buggy and asked for his buggy whip. Ulysses hadn't spoken one word to his friends or the white men. His calmness upset Villepigue even more. Ulysses gripped his mule and braced himself for what was to come. The frightened mule tried to run as Villepigue charged back toward the side of the buggy. He struck Ulysses with the whip, still holding his pistol in his left hand. Ulysses remained silent as this forty-year-old stranger continued to whip him. Henry Villepigue delivered a final slash to the left side of Ulysses's face and returned to his own buggy.

Ulysses looked around and saw that everyone had gotten out of the road and into the cotton patch. He touched his face and felt the blood seeping from his wound. Ulysses was a practical young man. He didn't address or even look at Henry Villepigue, who went on to Albany as if nothing ever happened. He didn't say a word to Lillie Bell or any of the other witnesses. He went up to a nearby house and asked for some turpentine to put on his gash. He returned to the buggy, continuing his silence, and led everyone back to Charlie Givens's house.

Charlie Givens asked what happened when he noticed the glistening wound on Ulysses's left cheek and the dried tears on the faces of the Givens sisters. Ulysses explained his run-in with H.J. Villepigue, and recounting it probably made the altercation seem silly. In the moment, Ulysses would've been too busy getting slashed to notice the ridiculousness of harming someone because of a traffic concern. In hindsight, it's truly unbelievable.

After nearly two hours of sitting in amazement, Ulysses decided to get himself together and go on home. The sun was close to disappearing underneath the horizon when he reached the Gilbert Landing Road. The Goolsbys had a large, beautiful home and plantation near the Pleasant Grove Methodist Church, which white people attended. Ulysses mentally prepared himself for his father's reaction as he put his mule in the lot. Inside the house, he found his mother, Mary M. Goolsby, in the kitchen.

Mary's father was the late Charles J. Hutchins, who at the time was one of the few Black landowners in Early County who kept his property until his death. It had been three years since his passing, and in his will, he left 50 acres of land to each of his surviving children. Mary and her twin sister, Martha A. Mozee, may have been the only Black women to own that much land at that time in Early County. Mary had already purchased 524 acres of land before she received her inheritance, as well as several town lots in Blakely. She also owned a large, beautiful house in which she raised her sons. Ulysses had three younger brothers, but only Roosevelt and Nathaniel were

Mary M. Hutchins Goolsby. *Family photo.*

Martha A. Hutchins Mozee, likely with her oldest son, Maslon Mozee. *Family photo.*

Roosevelt Goolsby. *Family photo.*

Right: Charlotte Law Hutchins. *Family photo.*

Opposite: Nathaniel Hawthorne Goolsby. *Family photo.*

home with Mary when he returned after the incident. His brother Mike was not home and neither was their father, Grandison.

Ulysses told Mary everything that happened, and all she could do was cry. Mary was born only four years after the end of the Civil War. It was heartbreaking to know that her family had survived slavery and Reconstruction only to be confronted with Jim Crow. Mary knew that Ulysses was not attacked solely because of road rage, but because the joy, wealth and freedom of a Black boy was offensive and threatening to many white men. This was especially true in 1915, the same year that *Birth of a Nation* was released, and even more true in Early County, Georgia, far away from any urban areas, where white people were more accustomed to seeing successful Black families.

After Ulysses spoke to his mother, he went back out to feed the mule and the hogs and felt the sensation of emotional exhaustion wash over him. He carried himself inside to lay across his bed, not knowing that it would be his last time sleeping there.

Meanwhile, people in the community were already discussing what happened between Ulysses Goolsby and Henry Villepigue on the Howard Landing Road. Word reached the ears of Ulysses's grandmother Sarah Law Goolsby. She was at the home of her sister Charlotte Law Hutchins when she heard what happened. Sarah's son Grandison was there as well but wasn't aware of what had occurred. She confronted her son, troubled by the family talking and laughing while Ulysses had his face split in half.

Grandison was troubled as well after hearing what his mother was saying. He knew that he had to confront this white man and that he might be killed in the process. Grandison looked up into the ceiling and started praying to God. When he was finished, he told his cousins to be prepared for anything, but he couldn't have known what was to come.

2
SELF-DEFENSE

On the morning of Wednesday, December 29, Ulysses was awoken by the cries of his father. Grandison wanted to know each detail of what occurred directly from his son. Ulysses repeated the events from the previous afternoon, but Grandison was not satisfied. He asked if Ulysses had done anything to upset Henry Villepigue in the past. Grandison was not familiar with this man and believed that he needed to get to the bottom of the issue, one way or another.

Mike Goolsby, the second-oldest son after Ulysses, heard what happened as well. Grandison explained that he was going to pay Villepigue a visit and that Ulysses and Mike were coming with him. Both brothers expressed their unwillingness to be a part of this confrontation.

Ulysses pleaded, "I don't want to go. The man tried to kill me for nothing, and I don't want to meet him ever again."

Grandison reaffirmed, "You must go," and ordered the boys to eat breakfast quickly while he hitched up the mule to the buggy.

As they headed out, Ulysses noticed that Grandison was driving the mule into town. After seven miles going southeast on the Fort Gaines Road, they were in the city limits of Blakely, far away from where the incident had occurred. Grandison stopped in town at multiple places before finally driving the mule back toward Pleasant Grove. He visited Andrew Jackson Singletary's commissary store, Elvin Booth Hamilton's hardware store and the home of Joseph Sydney Sherman on River Street. The boys had no idea what business he had done in town, and they didn't ask. It was later reported

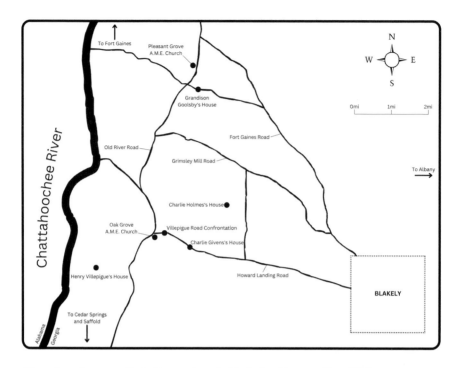

Map of northwestern Early County, based off of a land lot map from 1911.

that Grandison was there purchasing several rounds of ammunition. Others claimed that he was just visiting his white friends in Blakely and asking for advice. Supposedly, they encouraged him to confront Henry Villepigue and straighten the matter out.

After about ninety minutes of driving back west, Grandison stopped the buggy again, this time at a familiar place. They were at Charlie Givens's house on the Howard Landing Road. Grandison called out for Mr. Givens from the right side of the buggy. Charlie Givens came to the door.

"Is your father there?" Grandison asked.

"Yes, he is," Charlie replied. Grandison asked him to tell Mr. Givens to step outside. None of the Goolsbys got out of the buggy.

Mr. Givens went out toward the road to see what they wanted. Grandison asked if he could show them how to get to Henry Villepigue's house. Mr. Givens didn't waste much time answering. He was not feeling well and did not want to get involved. He asked his son to show them instead. Charlie agreed, went to his lot and caught his sorrel mule to ride behind the Goolsbys' buggy.

It was only two miles to the Coachman plantation, where Villepigue lived. Grandison used this opportunity to lecture the three young men about how to stay out of trouble. Charlie was significantly older than Ulysses and Mike, but Grandison thought that he could impart some wisdom to him too. In Black communities, it's never too early or late to discuss the "appropriate" way to address white people. Grandison, being born in 1869, was from an era in which racial confrontations almost always ended in death. He saw the advancement of colored people during Reconstruction and the swift reversal of those strides. He told them that if Ulysses was wrong in the matter, he would whip him for causing trouble with a white man. Ulysses could have lost his life, and Grandison was clear on making that point to him.

They pulled up to Henry Villepigue's house after an hour of riding. He lived on a private road, in a modest house with a porch and a fence. Grandison turned the mule and buggy around so that they were facing the direction they came from. He called out to Villepigue, stepped out of the buggy and walked around to its left side. He rested his hand on the rear wheel as Henry Villepigue appeared out of his door.

Henry had not yet responded to Grandison's hail. He walked toward the four "negroes" diagonally, staring them down as he breached the threshold of his front gate. As he got closer to the buggy, he noticed the wound on Ulysses's cheek.

"Ain't that the boy I whipped yesterday?" he asked.

The elder Goolsby responded, "Yes, this is my son, and I have brought him here to see if I could give you satisfaction."

"No!" Henry said. "Look out, I'm going to kill him!"

Grandison quipped, "You'll have to kill me first," as he reached under the seat of the buggy for his Winchester rifle.

Henry shot at the buggy before Grandison could retrieve his gun from under the croker sack that was covering it. Charlie's mule was startled by the shot, and he jumped off to lead her out of the way. Grandison returned fire as Henry fired two more shots with his pistol. Grandison shot again, and the bullet pierced Henry's arm, causing him to drop his pistol and run back toward his house. He called out for his wife to bring him a shotgun from inside the house.

Mike was struggling to hold the Goolsbys' mule as Ulysses contemplated a way to help his father. Grandison shot at Henry again as his wife opened the door of the house with another gun. Ulysses looked down at the sack his father hid in the foot of the buggy. He noticed a double barrel shotgun underneath. Ulysses grabbed it, stepped away from the buggy and fired twice. The Goolsby mule began to run when Ulysses stepped out, displacing the buggy about twenty feet before Mike got it stopped. The burlap sack that covered the guns fell onto the road.

Ulysses returned to the buggy as his father fired one more shot at Henry. Grandison joined his sons and started off driving, passing Charlie, who had been watching the commotion from a sixty-foot distance. The Goolsbys traveled one hundred feet away from the Villepigue residence when Grandison suddenly stopped driving and got out. He rushed back to fetch his croker sack, quickly returned to the buggy and took the reins.

Henry Villepigue barely made it into his house before he collapsed on the floor. His wife, Irene, went to the window to see that Grandison had left and come back. She looked at her husband's wounds and ran out through the back door to get help. Irene, five months pregnant, ran through the fields until she came across one of the laborers. She asked him to send for a white man, Marion Mosby McCullough, who was nearby hauling some wood on the plantation. By the time Irene returned to the house, Henry was dead, and Grandison, Ulysses, Mike and Charlie Givens were long gone.

Marion and some of the laborers entered the house and saw Henry lying on the floor in the hall. They picked up his body and laid it across the bed in the next room. Marion went back outside to get more help. As he was walking out of the yard, he saw Henry's pistol on the ground. He picked it up and saw that it had been fired several times. Marion continued on to Blakely, where he requested the assistance of John Oscar Bridges and Mayer Cohen. It was just after dark when he returned to the plantation with the other two men to inspect the body and dress him for burial.

The body was carried to the home of Nettie Coachman, sister-in-law of Henry Villepigue's boss. Nettie was the former Mary Jeanette Bridges, widow of Herbert Coachman. Herbert's brother Edwin owned the plantation where Henry Villepigue lived but took up residence in Clearwater, Florida, where he met Henry and Irene Villepigue. It hadn't been much time since the Villepigues relocated to Georgia, and Nettie Coachman was the closest thing to family that Irene could find.

Nettie lived on the Howard Landing Road just outside the city limits of Blakely. Her father, William Zachery Taylor Bridges, a Confederate soldier, was living with her when Irene showed up with Henry's body. Nettie's son, Lane Coachman, was with Henry when he first attempted to kill Ulysses Goolsby the day before. Her brother, John Oscar Bridges, was one of the men who prepared the body for burial. It didn't take much time for Irene's

Thomas Jackson Howell. *Early County Museum.*

outcry to spread to the white citizens of Blakely: "Three negroes shot my husband in the back and killed him! They shot at me too!"

Sheriff Thomas Jackson Howell was summoned. He immediately organized several searching parties, tasked with catching the Goolsbys dead or alive. The sun was setting by the time the mobs reached Grandison's home. They did not find him or his sons, and they advanced to search every "negro" residence near Pleasant Grove. Grandison's neighbors were his own sisters, Fredonia Harris and Beulah Crews, as well as his sister-in-law Martha Mozee. Their husbands and their children were all in grave danger. They watched in terror as droves of white men tore through their homes looking for their relatives.

Grandison had already pleaded with his family to vacate the area in expectation of what was coming. "Get off this place!" he screamed at his siblings and cousins, but they were hesitant to leave him there alone. He repeated himself several times, going to all of the family homes and explaining what happened, but by the time he finished telling everyone, the mob was already on the plantation.

A battle ensued as one of the mobs ventured farther north along the Old River Road. Shots rang out as groups of both races converged only a few hundred yards south of the Pleasant Grove African Methodist Episcopal Church and a few hundred yards north of the white Pleasant Grove Methodist Church. Until this dreadful night, the Pleasant Grove neighborhood may well have deserved its moniker. When the gunshots stopped, the crowds scattered throughout the dirt road in between the two churches. One of the bodies left in the dirt was that of Simon Goolsby, Grandison's youngest brother. He was dead.

3
BLAKELY ON FIRE

On Thursday, December 30, a spirit of mourning brooded over Early County, strong enough to disturb the soil of the AME cemetery where Simon would soon be buried. Mobs resumed their witch hunt once news spread that the wrong Goolsby was killed. Simon was thirty-two years old and had no children but was survived by a wife, Laura, and three stepchildren: Lessie Mae, Clarence and Carrie Belle Bass. Their home was still searched for Grandison, even as they were grieving their loss. Laura hid her son under the floorboards of the house to keep him safe, only opening a board every few hours to drop some food for him.

Henry Villepigue's body was already on its way to his funeral in Griffin, Georgia, as angry posses rampaged through the river sections avenging the death of their skinfolk. They ventured out toward the home of Grandison's first cousin Early Hightower. He refused to let the white men enter the cabin and attempted to defend his home with gunfire. The mob riddled the cabin with bullets and stormed inside. A body lay dead on the floor, later identified as Early Hightower. He was thirty-five years old, the son of Preston Hightower and Delia Law White. The mob of white farmers proved to be a relentless lynching committee, showing no remorse for the fallen Black men. Early Hightower had lived most of his life with his maternal aunt Charlotte Law. Charlotte and her six children were not there during the raid but hiding at Alfred Hutchins's house on the plantation of Jefferson Davis White.

Except for Henry Villepigue, none of the white people had been injured in this ordeal, yet. Their resources seemed infinite as more groups traveled in from other places to join the sheriff's search for Grandison Goolsby. Governor Nathaniel Harris, a former Confederate soldier, issued a proclamation offering a reward of $250 for the apprehension of Grandison, Ulysses and Mike. Although he specifically stated that they would need to be captured alive and tried in court to validate a reward, the statewide notification from Atlanta had various independent posses in a murderous frenzy.

Members of the posse that killed Early Hightower felt no shame as they ventured east on the Grimsley Mill Road. Word came that the Goolsbys had been seen hiding near the plantation of a white man named Robert Toombs Sirmons. He was known as "Dick," even though his name was not really Richard, and he was rumored to be the illegitimate son of John Gilbert, who owned the land that Grandison was born on in 1869. Dick Sirmons led the lynching mob to the residence of Charlie Holmes, who was known to be a friend of Grandison. They searched his cabin but did not find their target. The posse turned their pistols and rifles on Charlie Holmes and questioned him.

"Tell us where he is or meet your death!"

Reluctantly, Charlie gave them the answer they were waiting to hear. He explained that Grandison was hiding in the loft of the house but that Ulysses and Mike were hiding in a different cabin nearby. Members of the posse started out toward the other cabin immediately upon hearing this information.

Top: Laura Ross Bush, the widow of Simon Goolsby. *Family photo.*

Bottom: Clarence Bass, the son of Laura Ross Bush from her first marriage. *Family photo.*

Opposite, top: Nathaniel Edwin Harris, the sixty-first governor of Georgia. *Georgia Institute of Technology.*

Opposite, bottom: Robert Toombs "Dick" Sirmons, Maggie Knight Sirmons and their children Lois (*left*) and Vesta Sirmons, circa 1907. *Ancestry.com.*

Grandison Goolsby also heard these words from the concealed loft and so began his Hail Mary. He kicked out a board in the wall and fired into the crowd several times, striking Ollen Barbee Hudspeth in the head and Samuel Lee Pittman in the arm. Grandison was using Mauser rifle bullets to defend himself, but he did not have enough to subdue the white men trying to kill him. The injured possemen were carried into Blakely for medical assistance as the rest of the mob ordered Charlie Holmes to set fire to his home. He realized he had done all he could to help Grandison. If he didn't follow the order, he knew he would be killed and they would burn the house themselves.

Charlie Holmes wanted to stay alive for his wife and children, who were hiding in the woods. He obliged the lynch mob and torched his own home, which he had worked hard to afford. Grandison evacuated the scorching flames, only to be met with an immeasurable number of bullets. Charlie Holmes cried as he dragged the dying body of his friend away from his burning house. Grandison exhaled his final breath as the mild evening air began to fill with smoke. He was forty-six years old.

Several other structures were lit on fire in Blakely and at Pleasant Grove. An aerial view of Early County that night might've looked like a family of lightning bugs in a tree, until the streams of smoke rose high enough to form a dark cloud, consubstantial with the feelings from earlier that morning. The lynching mobs convened in the midst of Black grief to proudly account destroying Charlie Holmes's house, three Black fraternal lodges and one specific cabin, in

which the Goolsby brothers were shut in and burned alive. The white farmers rejoiced and spread the news: Grandison, Ulysses and Mike Goolsby were dead.

4
THE AFTERMATH

The smoke was still rising off the ashes of the buildings Friday morning as the front page of every newspaper in the country focused on Early County, Georgia. There were less than twenty-four hours left until 1916, and the notoriety made for a strange New Year's Eve. Black people asked their white friends for permission to sleep on their porches the night before. Those who stayed in their homes were urged to keep all their kerosene lamps extinguished overnight, as if they weren't home. They dared not roam the streets for any purpose. The manhunts had ceased, but there were still armed men patrolling the roads, itching for the slightest reason to get trigger happy.

The embers started to cool, and deputies were sent to recover the bodies of Ulysses and Mike Goolsby. They had already retrieved the bodies of Grandison Goolsby, Simon Goolsby and Early Hightower and dropped them at the front porch of Sarah Goolsby, where they lay unceremoniously through the night. In a mixture of terror and grief, she and her remaining family members quietly carried the bodies to Pleasant Grove for burial. Reverend Boston Scott whispered a short funeral service, reading from his Bible while others were on watch for the lynching mobs. They quickly inhumed the corpses without headstones or proper rites, as if they were cats and dogs. Meanwhile, those searching through the ashes for Grandison's sons discovered something that the Goolsbys already knew. There was no evidence of human remains in the debris of the cabin where the brothers were supposed to have been burned alive.

Right: Edward "Shane" Jewell. *Family photo.*

Below: Martin "Hash" Jewell, Leola Jackson Jewell and their children, from left to right: Benjamin Franklin, Curtis, Martin, Eva and Perlia Jewell, circa 1911. *Family photo.*

The posses knew that they needed to start the hunt again, but this time, they had to be quick. If the brothers were alive, they may have had a full day's head start at escaping the area. An investigation led the sheriff to believe that the boys were last seen with Martin "Hash" Jewell on Wednesday night. With guns to their heads, Hash and his nephew Eddie Jewell confessed to concealing Ulysses and Mike. Grandison sent his sons to the Jewells with the specific instructions of carrying them safely to relatives in Cedar Springs, a town at the other end of the county. Sheriff Howell promised to spare Hash and Eddie's lives if they told which relatives took custody of the Goolsbys.

Even so, the Jewells were hesitant to disclose the identity of the Goolsby concealers. They had brought the brothers to the home of Edmond Law Jr., who lived on the humongous Hudspeth Plantation. Ed Law's nephew Early Hightower was one of the men slain during the affairs of the previous afternoon. Ed's sister was Sarah Goolsby, who had just buried her sons Simon and Grandison. Hash Jewell did not want the Law family to suffer any more losses. Hash was born in Clay County, Georgia, but his father was enslaved by the Grimsley family, whose reach spread throughout both Early and Clay Counties. The Laws were enslaved by Robert Yelldell, a close associate of the Grimsleys, connecting them to the Jewells since antebellum times. Decades later, Hash was faced with fatal perils and left with no choice but to save his family from the state-sanctioned murderers at his doorstep. He gave Sheriff Howell Ed Law's name, and his life was spared as promised. Instead of death, he and his nephew were taken to jail.

The searching parties didn't waste any time leaving for Cedar Springs, determined to do to Ulysses and Mike what had been done to Grandison and Simon. The Hudspeth Plantation was over a dozen miles south of the area that had been searched in the days prior. It was some three thousand acres of fertile farmland owned by Julius Emmitt Hudspeth, a young grocer, and his mother, Martha Hudspeth. Julius's first cousin Ollen Barbee Hudspeth had been injured the night before by one of Grandison Goolsby's bullets, and the entire Hudspeth family was more than happy to help vanquish the Goolsby brothers.

The lynching mob was met with disappointment once it located Ed Law's cabin. Ed lived there with his wife, Rena, and his two adopted sons, Alto McCoy and Precious Hall. Ulysses and Mike Goolsby were long gone. Precious attempted to defend his sixty-eight-year-old adoptive father, and he lost his life in the process. He was twenty-one years old. Ed was tortured until he admitted to hiding his grandnephews in his cabin and bringing them seven miles south to Saffold, an unincorporated community in Early County that housed an Atlantic Coast Line train station. The depot at Saffold was essentially on the Alabama border, confirming the posse's fear that the Goolsby brothers made it out of Georgia. Edmond Law was executed for helping them escape, and the mob went on to continue their rampage.

As they returned from the county's southwestern corner, the rest of the populace did their part to fuel the widespread pandemonium of misinformation. The first rumor claimed that secret papers were found on

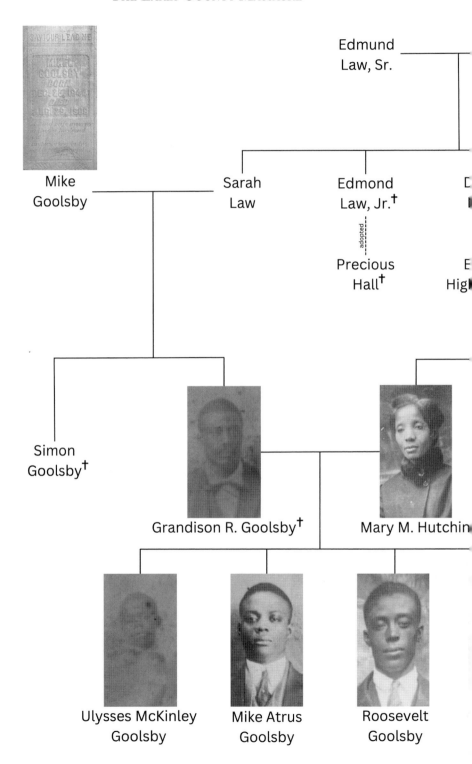

Edmund
Law, Sr.

Mike
Goolsby

Sarah
Law

Edmond
Law, Jr.†

adopted

Precious
Hall†

Simon
Goolsby†

Grandison R. Goolsby†

Mary M. Hutchin

Ulysses McKinley
Goolsby

Mike Atrus
Goolsby

Roosevelt
Goolsby

Five descendants of Edmond and Hulda Law were killed in the Early County Massacre.

the body of Simon Goolsby when he was killed Wednesday night. These papers were supposedly from a lodge book that detailed the orders for members of a Masonic lodge that the Goolsbys attended. Word spread that the orders specifically delegated Grandison, Ulysses and Mike to murder Henry Villepigue. The lynching mobs set fire to any Black lodge they passed during their searches late Thursday night and all day on Friday. One lodge building was dismantled by its members to prevent its burning, as it was very close to their homes. When 1915 ended, there was not one Black lodge standing in Early County, Georgia.

The gossipers also were spreading inaccuracies about Grandison's fiery death. In addition to the reports that his sons were burned to death, it was circulated that Charlie Holmes was killed for hiding Grandison in his loft. Charlie Holmes had not been seen because he was sitting in jail, along with Martin "Hash" Jewell and Eddie Jewell. The newspapers also claimed the death of "Wingate Harrison," misspelling the name of Grandison's brother-in-law George Winget Harris. George and his wife, Fredonia Goolsby Harris, were alive and well and eventually migrated to Cleveland, Ohio.

Late Friday night, another falsehood incited the fever pitch of white aggression. Someone telephoned Sheriff T.J. Howell to tell him that a crowd of Black people had gathered around the home of Hamilton Hayes Grimsley to avenge the deaths of the Goolsbys and the Laws. Armed white men across both Georgia and Alabama were alerted and asked to come save this white family. Meanwhile, there was absolutely nothing going on at H.H. Grimsley's house. Two hundred men arrived in automobiles at the quiet scene, surprised by the anticlimactic environment. They used the opportunity as a conference of the searching parties, sending cars toward the railways in Greenwood, Florida, and Montgomery, Alabama, on a hunt for the Goolsby brothers as 1915 came to a close.

5
MISSISSIPPI

After two and a half weeks on the run, Ulysses and Mike Goolsby were in dire straits. They made it to Cleveland, Mississippi, where work was scarce, and their funds quickly ran dry. They were following the footsteps of their Uncle App, who also escaped to Mississippi after being accused of murder several years prior. Alpheus Goolsby was the second-oldest child of Sarah Goolsby after Grandison. He supposedly killed Mariah Simons Igles on January 18, 1908. App was thirty-four years old when he became a fugitive, but Ulysses and Mike were only eighteen and sixteen, respectively.

Ulysses became desperate and tried to get a message to their father, having no knowledge of how Early County, Georgia, burned in their absence. He wrote a letter, asking for ten dollars and expressing a hope to return home. As gullible as it seems, at least Ulysses had the sense to sign with a fake name and address the letter to a neighbor. Unfortunately, the post office in Blakely caught on to the suspicious message and Sheriff Howell sent a deputy out to Mississippi to investigate its origins on Friday, January 21, 1916.

Lawton Carlyle Hobbs was a thirty-two-year-old grocer turned city marshal when he got his orders from the sheriff. Catching the Goolsby brothers meant that he would collect the reward money from the governor, so he was happy to head out to Mississippi. The lynchings were over in Early County, but the people were still angry even after three weeks. Sam Pittman, one of the white mob members shot by Grandison Goolsby, had his arm amputated at a hospital in Dothan, Alabama. The shot broke his arm, and the injury seemed minor at first, but it didn't heal correctly. Farmers in Early County rallied together to raise money for Sam, and their thirst for vengeance grew.

Black citizens in the area were still on edge and filled with fear. Charlie Holmes had become "mentally deranged" after being forced to set his home on fire with his closest friend inside. His father, prominent Black educator Jacob Holmes, pleaded for help. Sheriff Howell used the opportunity to take Charlie into custody for his "protection," charging him with accessory after the fact to murder.

Jacob Holmes was born in 1845, enslaved by Anthony Hutchins, who also enslaved Grandison Goolsby's father. Jacob was eventually bequeathed to Anthony's son-in-law Dr. Gamaliel Wyatt Holmes. Jacob's father was enslaved by Anthony's other son-in-law Martin Taylor Alexander. Yet another son-in-law was James Freeman, grandson of Robert Yelldell and heir of his enslaved population, which included Grandison's mother. The prominent white families in Early County treated Black people like property and traded them like poker chips. Inadvertently, they created some tight-knit relationships among the people they enslaved that held strong seven decades later.

Grandison Goolsby was the Worshipful Master of the Prince Hall Masonic Lodge in Blakely, Georgia, at the time of his death. Charlie Holmes was the Secretary, and their lodge, Starlight No. 95, was on a tract of land at 218 Jackson Street. The lot was deeded to Jacob Holmes in 1893, when he was the Treasurer. Jacob and Grandison had been members of the lodge since its founding in 1891. Grandison and the Holmes men were trustees of Pleasant Grove African Methodist Church, landowners, employers and highly respected men in the community. Grandison was also an officer in the Grand United Order of Odd Fellows and the Most Honorable Ruler of the Supreme Circle of Benevolence lodge at Pleasant Grove. These fraternal organizations exemplified the drive and perseverance of Black Americans at this time.

The incidents at the end of 1915 were not the first time that lodge buildings were burned in Early County, but this particular tragedy seemed insurmountable. Charlie Holmes was deeply tormented, not only by the loss of these great organizations but also by the loss of his friend. The lodge was rebuilt, but Grandison's presence and leadership was irreplaceable.

The white populace was determined to destroy any sense of wealth and success held by the Goolsby family and their associates. Three days before Lawton Hobbs arrived in Mississippi, Mary Hutchins Goolsby was forced

GOOLSBY VS. THE STATE OF GEORGIA

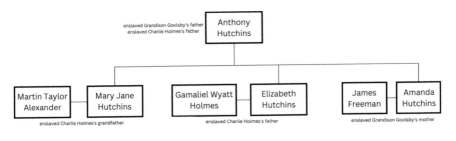

Top: The family tree of Anthony Hutchins Sr. includes people who enslaved the parents of both Grandison Goolsby and Jacob Holmes.

Bottom: This deed can be found on page 389 of Deed Book 29 at the Early County Courthouse in Blakely, Georgia.

to sell 375 acres of her large plantation back to Colonel Andrew Jackson Singletary and mortgage the other 200 acres. Andrew was the person that sold her 272 of those acres in the first place, just a few years earlier. Capturing Mary's sons, as well as Charlie Givens, were the final loose ends in the drive for retribution from the Black citizens of Early County.

Lawton Hobbs was able to recognize the Goolsby brothers pretty quickly once he got to Cleveland, Mississippi. In a way, they might have been grateful to be captured because they weren't going to survive much longer on their own. In reality, there was no end to the danger they could face coming back to Georgia. Lawton had to return Ulysses and Mike alive to receive the reward money, and he would receive it only once there was a conviction. He was certainly going to do everything in his power to keep them physically alive but made sure to kill their spirits by being the first to tell them what happened since they fled Early County.

Imagine being a teenager, raised in a community full of love and support, all of a sudden being put on a train by a granduncle to a land unknown. Spending three weeks there, longing to go back home, expecting everything to return to normal. Being apprehended by a white stranger who would get paid for the capture and imprisonment of his targets. Having to hear him recount the violent deaths of five close family members. Just imagine.

Lawton Hobbs sent a message to Sheriff Howell asking him to come to Mississippi. The sheriff was expected to leave Blakely on Tuesday, January 25, at 3:00 a.m., arriving in Cleveland, Mississippi, on Wednesday night. Then he would leave Cleveland on Thursday morning, arriving in Atlanta by the end of Friday, January 28. Sheriff Howell got permission to bring the Goolsbys to the Fulton County Jail in Atlanta, two hundred miles away from Blakely, to prevent the lynching mobs from killing them before their imminent convictions.

Ulysses and Mike knew at this point that their lives had been changed forever. With whatever time they had left on earth, their only solace was that they had each other. They had always been close, but their brotherhood was being tested in a way that was previously inconceivable, and they continued to endure.

6

DUE PROCESS

April was an exciting time in Early County because that's when the Superior Court judge for that part of Georgia came to town for two weeks. Folks couldn't wait to indict and convict Black people for whatever crime was convenient. White people were certainly convicted too, but out of all the people sent to the Georgia State Penitentiary from Early County in 1916, only one was white. Others may have been ordered to pay fines, as most of the prosecuted crimes were Prohibition and firearm violations. No one seemed to care about appearing impartial, proven by the presence of Ollen Barbee Hudspeth on the grand jury, which handed out the indictments. Ollen was shot in the head by Grandison Goolsby at Charlie Holmes's house less than four months prior. He was now presented with an opportunity to send the Goolsby brothers up for a trial with a guaranteed death sentence, making this judicial process simply an elongated form of lynching.

Ulysses and Mike were not the only cases related to the massacre that were brought before the grand jury. Charlie Holmes, Martin "Hash" Jewell and Eddie Jewell were brought up on the charge of accessory after the fact to murder. Charlie Givens had escaped to Bonifay, Florida, before the massacre started, but he was caught in February by the sheriff's brother Robert Lee Howell. He was brought up on the charge of murder, along with Ulysses and Mike, for killing Henry Villepigue. No charges were brought against the people who killed Grandison Goolsby, Simon Goolsby, Early Hightower, Ed Law or Precious Hall. Mary Hutchins Goolsby had

IN THE SUPERIOR COURT OF SAID COUNTY

The Grand Jurors selected, chosen and sworn for the County of *Early*
to-wit:

1. *J B Manly* FOREMAN.
2. *J H Bailey* 13. *R A Hall*
3. *A B Hudspeth* 14. *W J Bryant*
4.   15. *J M Manly*
5. *L L Brown* 16. *B M Lee*
6. *L L Lindsley* 17. *W H Tripp*
7. *Jno Strickland* 18. *A B Ward*
8. *J J Fur* 19. *C E Boyett*
9. *J J Wichzer* 20. *J A Highmore*
10. *Geo White* 21. *J E Benny*
11. *J B Dunn* 22. *W W Haddock*
12. *R S Rice* 23. *R C Singletary*

In the name and behalf of the citizens of Georgia, charge and accuse

Eddie Jewell and Hosh Jewell

with the offense of *Accessory after the Fact to Murder*

Superior Court

April Term, 191*6*

THE STATE
vs.
Eddie Jewell
Hosh + Jewell

(*accessary after the fact*)
(*to Murder.*)

B. T. Castellow
Solicitor-General.

No **BILL**

J B Manly
Foreman.

Prosecutor.

Above: Ollen Barbee Hudspeth was recorded as Grand Juror No. 3 on this indictment. Andrew Singletary's son Raymond was recorded as Grand Juror No. 23.

Left: The Jewell indictment was recorded as a "no bill," meaning that they were not tried on this charge.

Opposite: Bonifay is located in Holmes County, Florida, sixty miles southwest of Early County, Georgia. *Georgia Historic Newspapers*, Early County News.

no time to grieve or call for the prosecution of her husband's murderers. Since the capture of her sons in January, she had focused on supporting them through the legal process, all while continuing to raise her younger two sons as a single mother.

Mary hired Munday & Cornwell to represent Ulysses and Mike. The law firm operated out of the Kiser Law Building on Pryor Street in Atlanta. Its namesakes were William Chenault Munday and Gibson Hill Cornwell, prominent Georgia-born attorneys from Columbus and Monticello, respectively. W.C. Munday was the younger of the two but undoubtedly an experienced veteran who had been working at the Kiser Building since 1898. He passed the bar in 1893 at seventeen years old and moved to Atlanta shortly after. William represented several Black defendants in the early 1900s, most notably in cases concerning the Atlanta Race Massacre of 1906.

On September 24, 1906, a large group of Black people met in the Brownsville community of Atlanta to discuss how to defend themselves from white mobs that had been rampaging through the streets. The meeting was raided by police, and a gun battle ensued, leading to the death of an

---

Charlie Givens, the young negro man charged with piloting Grandison Goolsby and his boys to the home of Mr. Henry Villipigue when he was killed by the Goolsbys last December, was located and arrested at Bonifay, Fla., last week. He was brought back Saturday by Mr. R. L. Howell, who had "been deputized by his brother, the sheriff, to go for the negro. All parties who were concerned in the actual killing are now under arrest.

---

officer. All of the Black people there were arrested following the incident, and several dozen were charged with murder. William Munday was a part of the legal team that exposed the grand jury, which indicted sixty people without hearing any evidence at all. Apparently, the only witness called to testify before the grand jury was never sworn in, and all they did was read the names of the people indicted. William Munday and the other attorneys were able to get the indictments overturned after calling the grand jurors to testify before the judge.

Nearly ten years later, William C. Munday seemed like the perfect lawyer to represent the Goolsby brothers. Gibson H. Cornwell joined Munday's firm in 1911, two years after coming to Atlanta from practicing in Covington, Georgia. His brother-in-law was the chief deputy sheriff of Fulton County, where Atlanta is located. Between the two of them, Munday & Cornwell had considerable influence throughout the state of Georgia.

Veteran Attorney Passes

GIBSON H. CORNWELL.

Gibson Hill Cornwell. *From the Atlanta Constitution.*

On Wednesday, April 12, 1916, the April term of the Early County Superior Court was nearing its adjournment. In the preceding week and a half, the grand jury and judge had gone through many cases. The attorneys for the Goolsbys knew that they could not get a fair trial in Early County, so they filed a motion for change of venue. After a hearing, the motion was promptly denied by the judge. The attorneys had no intention of giving up, knowing that stalling the trial would be most effective considering temperaments. They immediately appealed the judge's decision, which required the motion to be heard by the court of appeals. This wouldn't happen until June, meaning that the trial couldn't start until October term.

Early County is a part of Georgia's Pataula Judicial Circuit, which at the time also included Clay, Miller, Quitman, Randolph and Terrell Counties. Judge William Charles Worrill had been the presiding justice since 1907. He was born in 1854 in Stewart County, Georgia, into a family of lawyers. His office was in Cuthbert, the county seat of Randolph County, and he held court in Early County only twice per year: April and October. Ironically, Judge Worrill's own son killed a man in 1911 and was arrested and released on bail, even after fleeing the state. Naturally, he was defended by three judges at his trial in 1912. A jury took only a few minutes to return a verdict of not guilty, and he was able to resume his life as a lawyer, later following in the footsteps of his father as a judge. As the older Judge Worrill denied all relief toward the Goolsbys, it became clear that they would not be afforded the same privileges.

By the end of June, Ulysses and Mike Goolsby had been sitting in a cell for five months. Atlanta's county jail was known as Fulton Tower and stood downtown at 208 Butler Street. Across the street at the state capitol, the Supreme Court of Georgia finally heard the motion from the Goolsbys' lawyers and ended their conferences on June 27, 1916. The tribunal was made up of six justices, led by Chief Justice William Hansel Fish. He was a native of Macon, Georgia, and came from a family of judges. He never finished law school, dropping out in 1871, but was still admitted to the bar a few months later. He was appointed as a judge in 1877 at the age of twenty-eight. The court also included Judges Beverly Daniel Evans, Joseph Henry Lumpkin II, Marcus Wayland Beck, Samuel Carter Atkinson and Hiram Warner Hill.

William Hansel Fish. *From* Men of Mark in Georgia, *Vol. 6.*

In a strange turn of events, the justices could not reach a majority on this decision. Lumpkin, Atkinson and Hill voted to let the Goolsbys stand trial outside of Early County, while the others voted to deny the appeal. In the event of a tie, Georgia law stated that the judgment remained as the lower court decided originally. In other words, Judge Worrill's ruling from April would stand, and the Goolsbys would have to return to Early County to face a jury in October. The decision was also made to have separate trials for

Yours sincerely,
J. W. Lumpkin.

JUSTICE HIRAM WARNER HILL, of the Georgia Supreme Court, who died Saturday after an illness of several months.

JUDGE MARCUS W. BECK

BEVERLY D. EVANS,
Who Has Been Appointed Associate Justice of the Supreme Court to Succeed Justice Turner.

Constitution Staff Photo—Bill Mason.

OLDEST AND YOUNGEST ON SUPREME COURT—The oldest and youngest members of the Georgia supreme court registered together yesterday at the convention of the Georgia Bar Association at the Biltmore hotel. Left to right are Judge Samuel Carter Atkinson, oldest member of the court; Chief Justice Charles F. Reid, youngest member; Frank D. Foley, of Columbus, president of the association, and Mrs. Grant Williams, of Macon, who was registering them.

Above: Samuel Carter Atkinson (*left*). *From the* Atlanta Constitution.

Opposite, clockwise from top left: Joseph Henry Lumpkin II. *From* Georgia and Georgians, *Vol. 4.*

Hiram Warner Hill. *From the* Atlanta Journal, *January 14, 1934.*

Beverly Daniel Evans. *From the* Atlanta Constitution, *March 11, 1904.*

Marcus Wayland Beck. *From the* Atlanta Journal, *January 21, 1943.*

the two brothers. This outcome was probably expected, but it's interesting to note that Ulysses and Mike were close to winning that appeal. One can only imagine how the following events would've changed if the trials were held somewhere else.

7

FRIDAY, THE THIRTEENTH

T he time finally came for the Goolsby brothers to return to the courthouse in their birthplace, Early County, Georgia, after waiting almost nine months for their trials. It was the second Friday of the Superior Court session convened by Judge William C. Worrill. He had already heard several cases on the charges of assault, burglary, larceny, carrying a pistol without a permit and three other murder cases.

The first case on the docket on the morning of October 13, 1916, was Superior Court of Early County No. 3111: *The State of Georgia vs. Ulysses Goolsby* for the murder of Henry J. Villepigue. Arguing for the prosecution was Bryant Thomas Castellow, the solicitor general for the Pataula Judicial Circuit of Georgia. He was a capable lawyer, having been a judge in Clay County, and he was completely prepared to use the full power of his current office against the Goolsbys, unintimidated by their Atlanta attorneys, William Munday and Gibson Cornwell. The court reporter was James Baugh Bussey, and it is his transcriptions of these trials that survive in the Early County Courthouse today.

Bryant Castellow had a variety of witnesses lined up to testify for the prosecution. Several were called to identify key locations and individuals for the jury, but they were not present at the death of Henry Villepigue. One of them was Edwin Horace Coachman, who wasn't even in Georgia at the time of the incident. He lived in Florida, but he owned the plantation that Henry Villepigue lived and died on. Edwin testified that he purchased the property from Julian Gaines Skinner, who bought it from Alfred Paulk,

Right: Bryant Thomas Castellow. *Underwood and Underwood*, Pictorial Directory of 74th Congress, *1935, Collection of the U.S. House of Representatives*

Below: The Early County Courthouse still stands in the center of Blakely, Georgia, adjacent to the last surviving original Confederate flagpole.

and that the land was interchangeably referred to as the Skinner Place, the Paulk Place and the Coachman Place.

Another witness was Early County sheriff Thomas Jackson Howell, who testified to his acquaintance with Henry Villepigue. The sheriff also testified to his knowledge of the Goolsby brothers and recounted going to

Mississippi to apprehend them. All of the men who examined Henry's dead body before it left his home were called to the stand as well. Marion Mosby McCullough testified that he picked the body up off the floor to place it on a bed but didn't count his wounds. John Oscar Bridges went into great detail, explaining that there was one bullet wound in Henry's right arm while the rest of his injuries were on his back. He described how to create a "cutshell" or "ringshell," a modified type of shotgun ammunition that he asserted caused the largest wound under Henry's shoulder blade. John described several other wounds that he identified as caused by either a rifle ball or a shotgun shell loaded with buckshot, citing his vast experience in weapons as credentials.

Meyer Cohen described the same wounds that John Oscar Bridges mentioned but admitted to his lack of experience with firearms. He was not able to tell which wound was caused by which gun. Dr. Cobb Rutherford Barksdale testified in the capacity of a medical examiner. He had been called to view Henry's body just before he was dressed for burial. Dr. Barksdale confirmed that Henry was shot near the elbow by a rifle or pistol ball that broke both bones in his forearm. He also observed the wound under Henry's right shoulder blade and stated in his professional opinion that this was the fatal injury. He did not examine any of the other wounds mentioned by the other witnesses.

The most damning prosecution witnesses were Irene Villepigue and Charlie Givens, who were both present when the shooting occurred. Once again, the county government had no desire to conceal their biases. Charlie may have felt coerced to testify for the state since he was also charged with this murder and had been imprisoned since his capture in February. Irene was the widow of Henry Villepigue, but at the time of the trial, she was likely engaged to Robert Aubrey Castellow. Robert was the first cousin of the prosecutor, Bryant Castellow. Irene married Robert two months later on December 20.

Bryant Castellow questioned Charlie Givens about various things. Charlie explained that he had known Ulysses Goolsby for three or four years. He stated that he was present at the death of H.J. Villepigue and that he was killed Christmas week with a breech-loaded shotgun and a rifle. Charlie told the jury how Grandison, Ulysses and Mike showed up at his house around 1:30 p.m. on December 29, 1915. He claimed that he did not see any weapons in the Goolsbys' buggy at that time. He was very clear about Grandison's expressed intentions in going to see Henry Villepigue.

"He said him and his boy got in a fuss and he wanted to go and see if he could straighten it out....He wanted to go see Mr. Villepigue, and if his boy had damaged his team in any way he wanted to pay for it."

Charlie spoke about how he followed behind the Goolsbys on his mule while they were riding in their buggy. He detailed the road leading to Henry's house and described the scene.

> *It is a private road that goes down to river. It passes in front of his house. Mr. Villepigue's house faces south. We were going west and the road let us in front of the house....When we rode up to Mr. Villepigue's we stopped....When Grandison called Mr. Villepigue, he turned the buggy around. Grandison Goolsby called Mr. Villepigue as soon as he stopped.... When he turned the buggy around, it was still in front of Mr. Villepigue's house. It was then about twenty yards from Mr. Villepigue's house. There was a fence around Mr. Villepigue's house. The gate is about ten steps from the front door of the house....Grandison Goolsby was about ten steps from the gate.*

Charlie explained how Henry eventually appeared in the doorway and walked outside without responding to Grandison's greeting. He didn't recall seeing a gun in Henry's hand, and he still hadn't seen one with the Goolsbys. That changed very quickly. Charlie claimed that as soon as Henry recognized Ulysses, he vowed to kill him on the spot.

> *And Grandison Goolsby said, "You kill me first!" and wheeled back to get his gun and as he done that—He reached in front of his buggy, down in the foot of the buggy. I had not seen the gun up to that time. Grandison Goolsby pulled out a Winchester rifle....It was pushed under the seat of the buggy and a sack spread over the stock—a croker sack, that would conceal it, I couldn't see it....When Grandison pulled his rifle out from under the seat of the buggy, Mr. Villepigue shot a pistol. I do not know where he got the pistol from. Mr. Villepigue was about ten steps, I reckon, from Grandison Goolsby when he shot. Grandison pulled out his rifle and ran back away from Mr. Villepigue's gun. Grandison Goolsby got about three or four steps further before he shot. This made them about fourteen feet apart. Grandison Goolsby shot at Mr. Villepigue. Mr. Villepigue shot the pistol three times, to my best recollection.*

Charlie went on to explain how after Henry's third shot, Grandison shot a second time and it struck Henry. He testified that Grandison continued to shoot as Henry turned around to run back toward his house. At this time, Charlie admitted that Ulysses Goolsby had stepped out of the buggy, retrieved a double-barreled shotgun from under his father's bag and shot at Henry once or twice as he retreated through his gate. This is essentially the only statement the jury needed to hear. Charlie didn't know if any of Ulysses's shots hit Henry, and he said Grandison shot one more time while Ulysses got back in the buggy. At that point, Henry was near the steps of his house, with his back still toward the Goolsbys.

On cross-examination, Charlie was interviewed by Ulysses's lawyer, William C. Munday. He asked Charlie to clarify for the jury that Henry Villepigue shot at the Goolsbys first and that no one had said anything at that point to indicate any animosity toward Henry. Charlie also testified that Ulysses didn't say a word throughout the entire incident and that Mike never touched any of the guns. Lastly, William Munday asked Charlie what he was in jail for. He responded, "I have not been notified of any charge. Have just been in jail."

Next, Solicitor Castellow called Irene Villepigue to the stand. Ironically, she was only a teenager herself, just months older than Ulysses Goolsby. She was born Irene Nunn in Jasper, Florida, and she married Henry Villepigue there on June 6, 1915. Henry was over twenty years older than her, born in August 1876. He was likely born in Beaufort County, South Carolina, where he lived with his mother, Caroline Stevens Villepigue, and his grandmother Mary Bostick Stevens. Mary's brother Richard Bostick was killed in 1858 by four people he held as slaves. Reportedly, they axed his head, burned his body and ground his bones into ash. It is possible that this family did not have a favorable opinion of Black people or even more likely, they had a grudge.

Irene may have shared these sentiments, based on the interview she gave to the *Macon Telegraph* just after Henry's funeral on December 31, 1915. She stated that Ulysses Goolsby caused the mass lynching of his family by getting in Henry's way on the road. She expressed gladness that the people who shot her husband had been "punished" and claimed that Henry had done nothing to provoke the incident. When she made those comments, she was under the impression that all the Goolsbys had been killed. She also explained that when the initial incident occurred, she was ending a holiday trip to Griffin, Georgia. She was there spending Christmas with Henry's sister Annie Dillard while Henry was still overseeing the Coachman

From the Victoria (Texas) Advocate.

A MASTER MURDERED BY HIS SLAVES.

Mrs. Naomi W. Sealy recently published an advertisement in the Advocate, offering five hundred dollars reward for any positive proof as to the wh reabouts of her son Richard S. Bostick, who disappeared mysteriously about the 9th of last January.

Suspicious circumstances led to the arrest of four of Mr. Bostick's negroes last week, who being sep-arately examined, confessed that they had mur-dered him. They state, that, having some three or four week's previous to the execution of the hor-rid deed, formed the plan of taking his life, they waited for a favorable opportunity. He had been riding on that day, and having been wet by a sud-den shower, he ordered the negroes to set fire to a large log heap, so that he could dry himself.—While he was lying before the fire, one of the men with an axe inflicted blows upon his skull which killed him, when they threw him upon the log heap. After the body was consumed, they pound-ed the bones into dust and mixed them with the ashes. The horse was killed, and together with the saddle sunk in a pond. The negroes showed the place where the unfortunate man was burned, where some buttons from his clothes were found, as well as some of the bones. The bones of the horse and also the saddle were found in the pond.

Among the circumstances which led to suspicion of the negroes, was the fact of their spending large sums of money. One of the party is a preacher, whose wife it is said, was instrumental in planning the murder, and earnest in urging its execution. The four assassins are in jail in Jackson county, awaiting their trial before the District Court.

Henry Villepigue's ancestor Naomi Sealy reported her son as missing after he was killed by people he enslaved. *From the* Anti-Slavery Bugle.

Plantation in Early County. Henry asked Irene to meet him in Albany, where he would pick her up and drive her home. He was on his way to get her when he assaulted Ulysses, and he returned home with his wife around noon the following day. In open court ten months later, Irene began to tell the rest of her experience that day.

> *I had been at home about two and one-half hours before the shooting. Mr. Villepigue brought me home. We reached home on that day about twelve-thirty o'clock in the afternoon. Just before the shooting, my husband was in the room with me. I do not remember when he left the room because I was asleep. The shooting waked me up. The shooting was in front of the house. From the house about twice as far as from here to the wall of the court room back there, I guess. When I waked up, Mr. Villepigue called me to carry him the shotgun. I got up and carried the gun to the front door of our house. There was a hall and a front porch to the house. I did not get any further than the front door of the house. When I got to the front door I could see what was going on in front of the house. I saw three negroes and my husband. One was sitting in the buggy. I could only see just one arm of him, they had the top turned so I could not see him. The other two were shooting.*

At this point, Irene pointed to Ulysses in the courtroom to identify him as one of the shooters. She also claimed that she first saw Ulysses when she and Henry were on their way home from Albany hours before the shooting. Irene said that Henry pointed him out as the boy he whipped the day before. She also made this claim in her newspaper interview from December. This statement is unsubstantiated and doesn't make much sense considering the travel routes taken by the parties involved that day. Unless Henry and Irene stopped in Blakely's town center while Ulysses and Mike were there waiting for their father, they couldn't have crossed paths before the shooting. However, Irene mentioned seeing only one "negro" at that time, and she claimed he ran into a house when he saw her and Henry. She was certainly mistaken about this, and these lies may have been crafted to suggest premeditation. Irene also alleged that Ulysses had both a shotgun and a pistol and that Grandison had a pistol. For some reason, she was under the impression that her husband had no weapon on him. According to her, he never fired at the Goolsbys and he had his back to them the entire time.

On cross, Counselor Munday asked Irene if she was certain Ulysses was the shooter. She admitted that she was not sure at all. She could not describe the guns used in the way that Charlie Givens did. She could not explain how the Goolsbys were holding the guns and she confessed that she simply didn't see what happened. Ulysses's lawyer also questioned her about the beginning of the shooting. He used this moment to remind the jury that she was asleep when the shooting began, and she could not testify as to who started the volley.

The prosecution rested their case, but the jury might have already made up their mind before the defense called their one and only witness: Ulysses Goolsby. With minor differences in the dialogue, Ulysses's account was consistent with Charlie's. The one major difference was that Ulysses did not admit to ever shooting a gun. He pleaded with the jury that he and his brother were only minors, not murderers. Ulysses was over eighteen, but at the time, the age of majority was twenty-one. At the end of his statement, Ulysses told the jury his father's last words to him and his brother before they were sent away to Mississippi.

"Boys, I would like for you to go on off, because I am satisfied they will kill me."

8
THIRTY MINUTES

The fate of Ulysses lay in the hands of twelve white men. The State of Georgia did not have a formal code of ethics for court proceedings in 1916. No one cared that the prosecutor's star witness was his first cousin's girlfriend. No one cared that one of the grand jurors was shot by the defendant's father. The trial jury likely included acquaintances of Henry Villepigue and people who participated in the lynching of Simon Goolsby, Early Hightower, Grandison Goolsby, Ed Law and Precious Hall. No one cared. The jury went into deliberations at 8:15 p.m. on October 13, 1916, and by 8:45 p.m., they had unanimously convicted Ulysses Goolsby of first-degree murder. At this time in Georgia, a first-degree murder conviction came with a mandated sentence of death. In thirty minutes, twelve white men agreed to end the life of a Black teenager.

Mike's trial ended up being on the following day, October 14. In addition to the witnesses from Ulysses's trial, these proceedings included testimony from Andrew Jackson Singletary, as well as the other white men Grandison spoke with in Blakely on the day of Henry Villepigue's death. Andrew, Elvin Booth Hamilton and Joseph Sydney Sherman all described how Grandison visited them that morning with Ulysses and Mike. They made it clear that they spoke only with Grandison and had no interactions with his sons. According to them, Grandison did not seem upset, and he spoke in a normal conversational tone. None of his words to them are in the witness statements, assumedly because they were deemed inadmissible by the court.

Mike was not at all implicated in the killing of Henry Villepigue but still forced to defend a charge of second-degree murder. His statement to the jury was particularly touching, even reminding the jury of his age just as Ulysses did.

> [My father] *was just going up there to talk it over with Mr. Villepigue. I was not going up there to harm anybody. And I had nothing to do with it, only my father made me go along with him up there. Therefore, we come on home and my father sent us off to keep from getting hurt; he sent us off and that is why we left home, and not for any crime that we had done....At the time that occurred, I was only fifteen years old.*

Regardless of his limited involvement, Mike was found guilty of murdering Henry Villepigue. Later that evening, Judge William C. Worrill sentenced Mike to spend the rest of his life in prison. He sentenced Ulysses to be hanged on November 17, 1916. The defense attorneys immediately made a motion for new trial, which survives in the Early County Courthouse today. The generic template reads:

> *The Defendant being dissatisfied with the verdict and judgment in said case, comes during said term of court, before the adjournment thereof, and within 30 days from said trial, and moves the court for a new trial, upon the following grounds to wit:*
>
> 1. *Because the verdict is contrary to evidence and without evidence to support it.*
> 2. *Because the verdict is decidedly and strongly against the weight of the evidence.*
> 3. *Because the verdict is contrary to law and the principles of justice and equity.*
>
> *Whereupon he prays that these, his grounds for a new trial, be inquired of by the court, and that a new trial be granted.*

Munday and Cornwell filed and served the motion upon Solicitor General Bryant Castellow, agreeing to present their arguments at Judge Worrill's office in Cuthbert in December. This saved Ulysses's life and deferred Mike's life prison sentence until these matters were resolved. The defense attorneys reserved the right to amend their motion with specific points and serve to Bryant Castellow within five days of the hearing.

On December 30, 1916, the attorneys and Judge Worrill gathered in chambers for the hearing, exactly one year after the lynching of Grandison Goolsby. William Munday and Gibson Cornwell amended their motion to include five errors made by the judge during Ulysses's trial. These errors occurred during two significant portions of the trial. The first four errors involved incorrect statements of law during the jury instructions before the trial. Apparently, Judge Worrill neglected to authorize the jury to consider voluntary manslaughter as a guilty verdict, only offering first- and second-degree murder as options. He also claimed that the jury could find Ulysses guilty of first-degree murder, even if it was Grandison Goolsby who shot Henry Villepigue in a spirit of revenge after meditation.

The last point was concerning an objection made by Solicitor General Castellow during the cross-examination of Charlie Givens. Counselor Munday was trying to ascertain more about the conversation between Grandison Goolsby and Charlie Givens while they were riding to Henry Villepigue's house, to show the jury that Grandison had no intention of harming anyone. Bryant Castellow objected to this question's relevance, even though he had been permitted to ask a similar question during his direct examination. The judge ruled in favor of the prosecution and sustained the objection, even though they opened the door to that line of questioning on direct. These are the grounds on which Munday and Cornwell requested a new trial, and their

HON. JAMES K. HINES.

Opposite, top: Stirling Price Gilbert.
Georgia Institute of Technology.

Opposite, middle: James K. Hines.
From the Atlanta Constitution.

Opposite, bottom: James K. Jordan.
From the Atlanta Constitution.

Right: Clifford Mitchell Walker.
Library of Congress.

arguments were convincing. However, Judge Worrill didn't think so, and he denied their motion on the spot.

The judge also denied the motion for Mike's new trial, which was based on different grounds. The defense complained that none of the evidence implicated Mike in the murder of Henry Villepigue, other than his physical presence at the scene. Neither Charlie, nor Irene, claimed that Mike fired any shots or provoked, supported or assisted Grandison in any way. Munday and Cornwell appealed the judge's rulings. One copy of the motion was to be stored in the Early County Courthouse, where it remained untouched for 104 years. A second copy was to be sent to the Supreme Court of Georgia, where it sat, also untouched, but only for the months it would take the justices to get through their caseload.

The Supreme Court of Georgia heard arguments concerning Mike's case on Monday, July 11, 1917. Including the judges and attorneys for both sides, fourteen jurists were gathered in one room at the state capitol. Chief Justice William Hansell Fish, Presiding Justice Beverly Daniel Evans, Marcus Wayland Beck, Samuel Carter Atkinson and Hiram Warner Hill were still judges on the panel. Joseph Henry Lumpkin II had passed away since the previous Goolsby appeal, and Judge Stirling Price Gilbert was appointed in his place.

Mike's representation at the hearing included his trial lawyers, Munday and Cornwell, as well as an additional firm: Hines and Jordan. James Kollock Hines and James Kollock Jordan were an uncle-and-nephew team with lots of experience. J.K. Jordan joined his uncle's Atlanta firm as partner in 1906 at the age of twenty-five. Opposing counsel included heavy hitters such as Pataula Circuit solicitor general Bryant Castellow, Atlanta lawyer Reuben Rose Arnold, Georgia assistant attorney general Matthew Campbell Bennett and Georgia attorney general Clifford Mitchell Walker. Clifford Walker was an alleged supporter of the Ku Klux Klan, and he later became the sixty-fourth governor of Georgia.

All the legal power in the world couldn't make this judgment stand. The judges unanimously agreed that there was no evidence to support a murder charge. Mike Goolsby was granted a new trial, two days before his birthday. At this point, he had been in jail for 530 days, and once again he had to wait until Early County's October term of court for trial.

Ulysses's case had yet to be heard by the Supreme Court of Georgia, even though his life was on the line. Those twelve white men had sentenced him to death the previous year, and now six white men had the power to affirm that sentence or temporarily spare his life by granting him a new trial. Defense attorney James K. Jordan enlisted in the army on August 17, 1917, to serve in World War I, but the other thirteen jurists finally reunited to defend, argue and hear Ulysses's motion on Friday, August 31.

Justice Hiram Warner Hill wrote the opinion of the court after the hearing. He stated that the exclusion of Charlie Givens's testimony due to the prosecution's objection was not grounds for a new trial because the testimony was immaterial and similar to what he was allowed to say during the direct examination. Hiram Hill also wrote that the court was not in error with incorrect statements of law, as Munday and Cornwell claimed. However, the justice did agree that the court was wrong to exclude the charge of voluntary manslaughter in the jury instructions, and his opinion was that the lower court's judgment should be reversed. Justice Stirling Price Gilbert disagreed with this, but that didn't matter. The other four justices concurred, and Ulysses was officially granted a new trial. He had been jailed for 581 days at this point, wondering which day he might be strung up. The trial jury took only thirty minutes to decide to end his life, but thankfully, they didn't have the final say. Unfortunately, this meant that the Goolsby brothers would have to go through the entire process again, with the possibility of garnering the same result. The fight was hardly over.

9
DÉJÀ VU

The October term of 1917 started off with a familiar circumstance: a full docket including both Goolsby brothers, just as it was one year earlier. The attorneys were fully prepared to retry and defend Ulysses and Mike on Monday, October 8, when things suddenly changed. The Early County Superior Court clerk, Robert Wooten Alexander, received orders to adjourn the court and dismiss the jurors. Judge William C. Worrill had fallen ill and was not able to resume court, which had started the previous week. The rest of the judge's autumn was occupied by cases in the adjacent counties of Clay, Miller, Randolph and Terrell, meaning that the remaining Early County cases would probably be deferred for several months.

In December, Judge Worrill was able to find another judge to hold a special session of Early County Superior Court. The Honorable James Parker Highsmith opened court in Blakely on Monday, December 10, 1917. James was a judge in Brunswick, on the other side of Georgia. He didn't waste any time and called the Goolsby trials on Tuesday, December 11. He was meticulous with jury selection, going through many men before approving the final twelve. After hearing the trial evidence, Judge Highsmith made the following statement regarding Mike Goolsby:

> On the former trial of this case, as in this, there was no evidence that Mike Goolsby did any act tending to produce the death of the alleged deceased, as charged in the bill of indictment, and the case was tried on the theory that he was responsible as a conspirator. The case was carried

to the Supreme Court, and the Supreme Court held in the case that the evidence did not authorize a finding against Mike Goolsby on that theory; that the evidence was insufficient to authorize the court to charge the jury the rule of law with reference to a conspirator. The Supreme Court having decided in this case that the court was not authorized to charge the jury the rule with reference to a conspiracy, this court would not feel justified in submitting the case to the jury again on that theory.... The only result that would follow would be a verdict of not guilty in so far as Mike Goolsby is concerned.

With this direction, Mike Goolsby was essentially acquitted of murder. Nearly two years after the death of Henry Villepigue and the Early County Massacre, Mike was free after spending 683 days in jail. So much had changed since he was forced to leave. His uncles and cousins had been killed. His father was killed. His last grandparent, Sarah Law Goolsby, died earlier in 1917. Even more bittersweet was that Mike had to leave his brother alone as he waited for his verdict.

The jury's decision on Ulysses finally came down on Thursday, December 13, 1917. At 10:30 a.m., the foreman declared Ulysses Goolsby guilty of first-degree murder once again. The testimonies of Solicitor Bryant Castellow's witnesses were too incriminating. Charlie Givens, who was still imprisoned in Early County Jail in 1917, and Irene Castellow, who married into Bryant's family, were all he needed to convict Ulysses. Of course, the defense attorneys prepared to appeal, but they needed to go about things differently this time. Meanwhile, Judge Highsmith sentenced Ulysses to hang on February 1, 1918.

Once again, Ulysses's life was saved by a motion for a new trial. The hearing with Judge Highsmith was on February 23, 1918. He denied the motion, forcing the defense attorneys to appeal to the Supreme Court of Georgia for the fourth time. Ulysses was alive but still in jail. This time, he was kept at Dougherty County Jail in Albany, Georgia. He registered for the World War I draft there on September 12 while still awaiting news from the appellate court. Finally, his case was called on October 16, 1918, and Counselors Munday, Cornwell and Hines returned to fight for Ulysses's life.

William Hansel Fish was still the chief justice of the Supreme Court of Georgia, but Beverly Daniel Evans was no longer the presiding justice. His last day in that seat was actually August 31, 1917, the same day he previously heard Ulysses's case. Marcus Wayland Beck was promoted to presiding

Walter Franklin George, the namesake of a well-known lake near Early County. *Library of Congress.*

justice, and Walter F. George was appointed to fill the vacant seat. Samuel Carter Atkinson, Hiram Warner Hill and Stirling Price Gilbert rounded out the rest of the panel on October 16, 1918.

All six justices agreed that Judge Highsmith made one small error during the trial: he talked too much. He overstepped a boundary in his charge to the jury in which he stated why Mike should be acquitted. Presiding Justice Marcus Beck said in his opinion that "the charge set forth was calculated to make upon the jury the impression that the trial judge was of the opinion that there was sufficient evidence to show a conspiracy between Mike Goolsby and some other party....

And if the jury believed there was a conspiracy, then they would be led to conclude, from what the court said and the evidence in the case, that the conspiracy was with no other person than Ulysses Goolsby."

The cases against Mike and Ulysses had the same jury, and the Supreme Court thought that the jury instructions from Judge Highsmith about Mike's verdict could have affected how they voted regarding Ulysses. Justice Beck concluded, "Inasmuch as this charge of the court contains an expression or intimation of opinion upon the facts of the case, it was error which requires the grant of a new trial."

With the complete concurrence among the justices, Ulysses's life was saved and he was granted yet another trial. He had to wait several months until April 1919 term of Early County Superior Court to be tried a third time, three years after his initial indictment. Ulysses's attorneys presented a justified homicide defense, citing *Dempsey Taylor vs. The State of Georgia* as reference. Dempsey killed a man named Abraham Benjamin Conger Sr. after an altercation in Tifton, Georgia, and was acquitted after two trials. Ulysses was quoted as saying, "I was seventeen years old; and I never give a white man a cross word. I had nothing in my heart against anybody. I never had as much as you could hold on a pin point against any white folks."

The Early County jury was not convinced, and Ulysses was convicted of first-degree murder for the third time. Just before sentencing on April 17, 1919, Judge Worrill was notified that his daughter Carolyn Strain died of chronic nephritis in Darien, Georgia, the day before. He immediately sentenced all the convicts and adjourned court to head to the funeral. May 30 was chosen as Ulysses's hanging date before Judge Worrill went to go bury his daughter.

As expected, Munday and Cornwell made a motion for a new trial, which postponed the execution. Judge Worrill denied the motion at a hearing on June 21, 1919, and the defense took exception. Ulysses was still waiting for the Supreme Court of Georgia to hear his case when he was enumerated in the Fourteenth Federal Census on January 16, 1920. He remained a prisoner in Albany, Georgia, at the Dougherty County Jail. It had been almost four years to the day since the Early County sheriff captured Ulysses and his brother in Mississippi. They were no longer teenagers but grown men who had experienced unspeakable horrors. Mike was now safe, but Ulysses's life was still on the line, and his worst fear was about to come true.

On March 9, 1920, the Supreme Court of Georgia affirmed Judge Worrill's ruling. Presiding Justice Marcus Beck was absent due to illness, but the other five judges were in full agreement: Ulysses Goolsby should be hanged.

10
OUT OF APPEALS

On Friday, April 9, 1920, Ulysses Goolsby found himself at the April term of Early County Superior Court for the last time in his life. This time, he was not there for a trial or for a hearing. There were no more appeals to be made with the courts. Ulysses was only there to be resentenced to hang. Judge Worrill chose Friday, May 7, and William C. Munday made notice of his application to the prison board to commute the sentence to life imprisonment instead of death. That was not enough to spare Ulysses's life. Munday needed to plead with Hugh Dorsey, the governor of Georgia.

Hugh Manson Dorsey was elected governor in 1916 and took office in 1917, as the Goolsby brothers were awaiting the results of their first appeal for a new trial. Dorsey agreed to postpone the execution until June 4, giving time for the Prison Commission Board to go over the case. On Friday, May 28, Commissioners Eugene Leigh Rainey, Robert Emmett Davison and Thomas Edwin Patterson considered the petition to commute the sentence. They denied it and ordered that Ulysses be hanged on June 4.

The headline on the June 3 front page of the *Early County News* read, "Ulysses Goolsby Will Hang Tomorrow." The subsequent article stated, "Ulysses Goolsby must hang tomorrow (Friday). His last chance for a commutation of sentence faded when Governor Dorsey on last Saturday declined to interfere with the court's verdict. The prison commission had on the day previous taken the same action. The Goolsby hanging tomorrow is the final chapter of the race riot which took place in this county some five years ago, which began with the killing of A.H. Villapigue, a white farmer of this county, by Grandison Goolsby and his boys, Mike and Ulysses."

The newspaper was so excited to report on the execution that they didn't even correct the name of the man Ulysses supposedly killed. Henry J. Villepigue wasn't even a farmer from Early County but an overseer who had only been in the county for a few months. Regardless of the reason, the people in Blakely grew excited for the hanging. Sheriff Thomas Jackson Howell prepared to do the honors himself.

On June 4, 1920, Ulysses woke up knowing that it was his last day on earth. He had been jailed in Georgia for 1,589 days. He survived whipping, shooting, lynching, escaping to Mississippi and being caught, being jailed and three murder trials. There was nothing else he could do but wait

Hugh Manson Dorsey. *Hargrett Rare Book and Manuscript Library.*

for the sheriff to bring him to his fate. But no one came for him. June 4 passed by, and he was still breathing and still in jail. Eventually, word came that Munday and Cornwell secured another respite from the governor due to newly discovered evidence that had to be reviewed by the Prison Commission.

The governor's respites lasted only for thirty days, and Ulysses was almost hanged in July and in August, even though the new evidence had not yet been heard. Eventually, the Prison Commission asked the governor to choose a final hanging date after their scheduled hearings in September 1920. Sheriff Howell received the following proclamation from Governor Dorsey:

Whereas, Ulysses Goolsby under sentence of death in Early County, Ga., the date of execution having been fixed for Friday, August 20th, 1920, has, through his Attorney, petitioned the Prison Commission and the Governor for a commutation of his sentence from death to life imprisonment and

Whereas, on August 11th, 1920, the Prison Commission have directed the following letter to the Governor:

"In re: Ulysses Goolsby, application for clemency. The attorneys for the applicant have made application for a rehearing on said clemency petition on the grounds of new evidence and additional affidavits sustaining their petition. Our next week for hearing applications will be the first week in September, and we would recommend that the Governor grant a respite so that said hearing may be had at the time."

Ordered: That a respite be granted and the same is hereby granted in the case of Ulysses Goolsby, aforesaid, from Friday, August 20th, 1920, until Friday, September 17th, 1920, and the sheriff of Early County is hereby directed to delay and postpone the execution of the sentence aforesaid until Friday, September 17th, 1920, on which date in the absence of any legal direction to the contrary, he shall proceed to execute the sentence of the court.

Hugh Dorsey was not a favorable figure in the weeks leading up to the new hearing. He was in a difficult position, even though he had declined reelection as governor. Dorsey had his eyes set on a seat in the U.S. Senate, and he had

JUDGE RAINEY PASSES AT HOME AT DAWSON

State Official Succumbs

Continued From First Page.

home here purchased the Dawson News.

Prior to being appointed a member of the state prison commission, he held various municipal offices here and other state positions.

He is survived by his widow; a daughter, Mrs. Brady Skelton, of Atlanta; a son, Clement E. Rainey, business manager of the Dawson News, and two grandchildren.

CZECH LEADER KILLS SELF.

PRAHA, Czechoslovakia, June 19. (AP)—Franz Stanek, 68, former president of the chamber of deputies and former member of the Czech cabinet, shot himself to death today in a local sanitarium. Officers said apparently he was depressed by an incurable illness.

JUDGE E. L. RAINEY.

Eugene Leigh Rainey. *From the* Atlanta Constitution.

Left: Robert Emmett Davison. *From the* Atlanta Constitution.

Right: Thomas Edwin Patterson. *From* Notable Men of Atlanta and Georgia.

heavy competition in Michael Hoke Smith and Thomas Edward Watson. Incumbent senator Hoke Smith had supporters who began circulating rumors that Governor Dorsey was going to save Ulysses's life. Dorsey wrote a letter to the people of Early County, explaining his postponements and that he had no intention of commuting the sentence.

> *After the case was right up to me, the Prison Commission recommended, in view of certain showing made by counsel representing this man, that he be given a further respite. I didn't have time to pass on the matter at that time. I, therefore, was compelled either to let this man hang without giving him a hearing, or defer to the recommendation of the Prison Commission and set the case over. While this man may deserve to hang, he is still a human being and the law provides that he may have recourse to the Governor. I have never yet permitted any man to hang until I had fully gone into the matter, and until I had permitted his attorneys to present their case in full....*
>
> *I am very sorry indeed if my disposition to give this man what I think he is entitled to under the law, and that showing which under the Constitution*

I feel I am sworn to give him, hurts me politically. But I'll just simply have to take the consequences....

I THINK I CAN ASSURE YOU THAT THERE WILL BE NO FURTHER RESPITES GRANTED, certainly not unless counsel show due diligence and facts that are so compelling that I could not deny to them further extension. It is very improbable that such a situation will arise.

It is not clear if the governor actually wrote all those words in capital letters, but that is how it was printed in the *Early County News* on September 2, 1920. The letter was sent to the newspaper by Blakely residents who claimed to be friends of Hugh Dorsey. Dorsey went on to explain in the letter that he did not yet know the facts of the case, and he urged the residents of Early County to remember that, even though they had been waiting for this execution for nearly five years.

On the morning of September 16, 1920, Sheriff Howell received a telegram that shocked the whole state. Governor Hugh Dorsey commuted Ulysses Goolsby's sentence to lifetime imprisonment with no explanation. The execution was canceled. Ulysses's life was truly saved for good.

This decision was highly upsetting to the residents of Early County, and even more upsetting to them was the rationalization of it that accompanied the announcement in the newspaper. In the *Early County News* on September 23, 1920, editor William Walter Fleming impartially printed the following rebuttal directed toward him:

In your paper of last week in referring to the fact that Governor Dorsey had commuted the sentence of Ulysses Goolsby from hanging to life imprisonment, you make the following statement: "The governor's action will be received with mixed condemnation and approval in Early county. The white element that foster the mob spirit will be greatly displeased, while the negro labor element and those dependent upon the contentment of the laborers will approve the governor's action."

Since you have taken it upon yourself to become the spokesman for the people of Early county, and announce for them in positive terms how they would regard this action of the governor, we propose to announce to them our opinion of your statement about the matter.

You can, no doubt, recall, Mr. Fleming, that this negro, with his father and brother, all heavily armed, went to the home of Henry Villipigue, which was several miles distant from any white person's home, and, in the presence of his wife, shot him to death.

This negro was tried three different times in this county, and found guilty without recommendation each time. Thirty-six citizens of our county said that he was guilty and should hang. Had they thought he deserved life imprisonment they could have given him that punishment. If your statement is correct, Mr. Fleming, those thirty-six men belong to the mob element of Early county.

The supreme court of Georgia, composed of six upright men, learned in the law, said that he was guilty and should hang. If your statement is correct, Mr. Fleming, they were fostering the "mob spirit" of Early county.

The Prison Commission of Georgia, composed of three upright and honorable gentlemen, said that he was guilty and should hang. If your statement is correct, Mr. Fleming they were fostering the "mob spirit" of Early County.

Did the white people of Early county want this negro's sentence commuted? You say that "those dependent upon the contentment of the laborers will approve the governor's action." That statement is not true, Mr. Fleming, and you made it, either through dense ignorance or from a desire to excuse the man whom you so ardently supported for the United States Senate in the recent primary. If you think you are correct, go among the employers of labor and ask them if they approve this action. We will here and now pay you a reward of $5 for every man who will sign his name to a statement that he approves this action. The truth is the people of Early county wanted the sentence pronounced on this negro by Judge Worrill carried out, and they are deeply resentful of this interference by Governor Dorsey.

Your statement is, in effect, that because our superior court sentenced this negro to hang, which sentence was affirmed by the supreme court, and which sentence the prison commission refused to interfere with, and because the people of the county wanted him hung, that that "fosters the mob spirit," and that the actions and desires of such people as you and Governor Dorsey discourages the mob spirit.

Had Governor Dorsey permitted the sentence of the court to be carried out, it would have had the effect of making the people confident that when a brutal crime, such as this, was committed, they could rely on the courts to inflict just punishment on the criminal, and they would have been willing to leave the matter to the courts, and instead of "fostering the mob spirit," the hanging of this negro would have discouraged it.

The thing that "fosters the mob spirit" is the very thing that Governor Dorsey has done, and which you have attempted to excuse, in this instance; and should Early county be so unfortunate as to have a similar crime committed in her borders again, there is almost sure to be an outbreak of mob violence for which Governor Dorsey will be directly responsible. The white people of Early county simply will not stand by and permit negroes to shoot down a white man in cold blood without indicting the severest punishment, and they will do so themselves, and it is our opinion that you, Mr. Fleming, have classified yourself incorrectly; you belong to the crowd which "fosters the mob spirit" in agreeing with the governor about commuting this sentence, while the folks who wanted the sentence of the court carried out belong to the people who believe in law enforcement.

There is something "rotten in Denmark" about this commutation. This negro was backed by the negro secret societies, and there is no doubt they furnished all the money that was required to save his neck. Everybody knows that if he had not been backed by some outside influence, that he could not have kept his case in court for five years, and then got a governor to commute his sentence. Did you ever know of an application for executive clemency being made where a petition was not gotten up among the citizens of the county where the crime was committed? You say certain people wanted his sentence commuted. Did any of them sign a petition to that effect? Did you sign it, Mr. Fleming? Would you have signed it if one had been presented, to you? Just come right out and let the people know if you signed such a petition, or would have signed it, if you had been asked.

This statement of yours, Mr. Fleming, is uncalled for, and unnecessary. There was no reason why you should rush to Governor Dorsey's defense, except to excuse yourself for your active support of him in the recent election. This statement is a reflection upon Early county, upon her courts, her juries, and her citizens, and if you ever did acknowledge you were wrong about anything, is a statement you will live to regret.

This was brought forth by Cleveland Hartley, who compelled several other citizens to sign their names to it, including Crawford Williams, Samuel Aristides Williams, Mack Curin Cobb, Andrew Dewey Jones, Durwood Newton McArthur, John Liston McArthur, James Rufus Askew, James Livingston Spurlock, Kirby Harris Moore, Lewis Floyd, John Thomas Durham, Howard McGee Moore, Mark Calhoun Sprouse, James Cornelius Balkcom, Emmett Edgar Tedder, Wade Washington Brunson, Thomas Mitchell Thompson and James W. Thompson. Cleveland Hartley was clearly an intense person, and he later shot himself in the heart after shooting his own son four times in Bainbridge, Georgia.

Of all the points made in this editorial, it was never mentioned that Ulysses's father, two uncles and two cousins were lynched by angry mobs. The writer spoke of William Fleming's "dense ignorance" or "desire to excuse," while completely ignoring that Early County was the leading Georgian county in lynching, save for Atlanta's Fulton County. It is not ridiculous to claim that the government fostered the mob spirit. Early County's sheriff was the one leading the posses that extrajudicially executed Simon, Early, Grandison, Edmond and Precious. A confirmed member of the mob that killed Grandison was on the grand jury that indicted Ulysses in the first place.

It's clear that a racial double standard prevailed in the mind of this poor soul. Governor Dorsey's letter to Early County had a striking difference when compared to all other literature concerning Ulysses Goolsby. Dorsey was the only person to refer to Ulysses as a human instead of as a "negro." Nearly fifty-five years after slavery, it was still a difficult concept to grasp for many that Black people were just as human as white people.

William Fleming's critic did have one valid point: Who paid for Ulysses' lawyers? Mary Goolsby was well-off when her husband alive, but without someone to work her land, poverty was imminent. Grandison Goolsby was in charge of several Black benevolent organizations that also served as insurance companies for their members. The societies had massive funds during this period of fraternal growth, and it is possible that they intervened to help Ulysses. He testified on January 1, 1917, that he was out of funds to pay his legal fees yet was able to afford two big-city law firms at his Supreme Court hearing later that year. Furthermore, Mary's brothers, John Morgan Hutchins and Charlie B. Hutchins, sold or mortgaged their farms in 1917. Those funds may have been used to assist the Goolsby brothers. It should be noted that various groups of Black Americans have always historically done the best they could to support one another. Because of their collective actions, Ulysses Goolsby was still breathing on September 18, 1920.

11

POSTMORTEM

November 17, 1916
February 1, 1918
May 30, 1919
May 7, 1920
June 4, 1920
July 23, 1920
August 20, 1920
September 17, 1920

Ulysses Goolsby was legally sentenced to die eight times within four years. Three illegal attempts on his life were made in December 1915. He was received by the state prison system to begin his life sentence on Wednesday, September 22, 1920. He was placed at the prison camp on Blacks Bluff Road in Floyd County, Georgia.

Governor Dorsey's reasoning for commuting the sentence was never disclosed in the media, but his clemency application records were filed at the Georgia Archives. The hefty collection contains letters from various Early County citizens calling for the hanging of Ulysses Goolsby, including Byron Collins, Eugene Collins, Mack Strickland, Sidney Winston Howell and even Raymond Singletary, son of Andrew Jackson Singletary. Raymond did admit to his close relationship with Grandison Goolsby in his letter but still stated that Ulysses should be killed.

Governor Dorsey received only one letter from a white person in support of keeping Ulysses alive. It came from Cyrus Raleigh Narramore, former Clay County sheriff and former Early County representative in the Georgia state legislature. Cyrus sent the letter to Ulysses's lawyer to be added to the petition for clemency. He described how no witnesses felt safe enough to testify on behalf of Ulysses at his trials. Cyrus also mentioned that he owned the farm adjoining the Goolsbys and described Grandison as a "good negro" and "polite to all people." He then described Henry Villepigue as "a desperate man beating and shooting at negros at the slightest cause."

Counselor Munday also included letters and affidavits from Ulysses's friends and family in the clemency application. Mary Goolsby testified that neither of her sons wanted to go with their father the day that Henry Villepigue died, which showed that Ulysses had no predetermined intent to kill anyone. She also said that people threatened to lynch her if she testified at the trials. Mike Goolsby said the same things in his affidavit, explaining how Sheriff Howell suggested he never return to Blakely after he was acquitted, preventing him from testifying at Ulysses's final trial.

Munday and Cornwell were also deposed by a notary public about their experience as Ulysses's lawyers. They discussed how they tried to employ lawyers in the Early County area to help them defend the Goolsbys. They were told that it would be suicidal for an attorney in southwest Georgia to join that defense team, and therefore Munday and Cornwell had to go through the jury selection and trial with limited information about the area. Governor Dorsey considered these affidavits to be sufficient evidence that Ulysses's trial was unfair and he should not have been found guilty of first-degree murder or sentenced to death.

Governor Dorsey had already made his decision by the time he read a special testimony from Charlie Givens. Charlie had moved to Newark, New Jersey, after spending three years in jail as a material witness for the prosecution. He was safely far away from Early County and decided to admit to being coerced to perjure himself on the stand. Charlie stated in a handwritten letter, "I am sorry to my heart that I had to swear against Ulysses but I had to do so to save myself because I was in danger."

Ulysses's lawyers worked a miracle gathering all these testimonies and getting the governor to postpone the execution until after the hearings. One might wonder how they were able to accomplish this. William C. Munday later became a judge and died in Atlanta in 1934. His obituary from the *Atlanta Constitution* contains a possible clue: Hugh Dorsey was a pallbearer at his funeral. This is evidence that Governor Dorsey and Munday may have been very close friends, and this could have been in Ulysses's favor. This could not have been planned in advance, as Munday was hired when former Confederate officer Nathaniel Edwin Harris was governor. Dorsey would leave a different gubernatorial legacy, chronicling the pandemic of racial injustice in Georgia and outlining the steps to take to remedy the problem in an iconic 1921 speech.

Other circumstances contributed to the uniqueness of this ordeal, such as the aforementioned wealth and fraternal support of the Goolsbys, the judge getting sick before the second trial, interruptions from World War I and the insistence of City Marshal Lawton Hobbs to remand the Goolsbys in jails far away from Early County, albeit solely for the purpose of receiving the reward money offered by Governor Harris. Any change in these events could have ended Ulysses and Mike's lives much earlier. Many other young men in similar circumstances did not have their lives spared.

On March 7, 1924, Mary Hutchins Goolsby died from diabetes at the age of fifty-four. Ulysses was still in prison. Despite a 1925 attempt by the NAACP in Rome, Georgia, to have him pardoned, Ulysses was enumerated as the prison cook in the 1930 Federal Census. On December 22, 1931, Ulysses was transferred to the Gilmer County Convict Camp in Ellijay, Georgia. On November 28, 1933, he was transferred to a state highway camp in Peach County, Georgia. He was a member of the Georgia chain gang, forced to build public roads and bridges in shackles.

Mike Goolsby had moved to Atlanta by 1918, when he registered for the World War I draft. He married Ada Mae Mapp of Greensboro, Georgia, in the early 1920s. They had several children and stayed in Atlanta until his death from a stroke on October 18, 1940. He was forty-one years old. Roosevelt Goolsby also moved to Atlanta, where he died on February 5, 1972, at the age of seventy. He named his son Granderson, after his father. Nathaniel Hawthorne Goolsby first relocated to Birmingham, Alabama, before moving in with his brother Roosevelt in Atlanta. Afterward, he settled in Los Angeles, California, where he died on September 6, 1969, at the age of sixty-four. He worked as a dry cleaner in each city he moved to.

It has not yet been determined when Ulysses McKinley Goolsby died. He was the oldest son of Grandison R. Goolsby and Mary M. Hutchins, who were married on January 23, 1895. He was faithful and obedient to a fault, having a great deal of love for his parents. Even with the full support of a strong community, his life was derailed because of the decisions of others and the failure to recognize him as a human being. He never had the chance in life to reach the full potential of a young Black man in his position. The

Above: M.A. Goolsby, February 8, 1922, likely in Atlanta, Georgia. *Family photo.*

Opposite, top: The grave of Mike Atrus Goolsby and Ada Mapp Goolsby in DeKalb County, Georgia.

MARRIAGE LICENSE.

State of Georgia, Early County.

By the ORDINARY of said County.

To any JUDGE, JUSTICE OF THE PEACE or MINISTER OF THE GOSPEL,

You are Hereby Authorized to Join

Grandison Goolsby & Mary M. Hutchins (col)

In the Holy Estate of Matrimony, according to the Constitution and Laws of this State; and for so doing, this shall be your sufficient License.

And you are hereby required to return this License to me, with your Certificate hereon of the fact and date of the Marriage.

Given under my hand and seal of office, this 22 day of Jan'y 1895—

J. B. Chancy [L.S.]
Ordinary.

GEORGIA, Early County.

I CERTIFY, that *Grandison Goolsby* and *Mary H. Hutchins* were joined in Matrimony by me, this 22d day of Jan'y Eighteen Hundred and Eighty 95 *G. D. Jordan* M. G.

Recorded: 8/14/90 *J. B. Chancy* Ordinary.

A. W. BURKE & CO. PRINTERS, MACON, GA.

Grandison and Mary Goolsby were married by Reverend Giles Dolphus Jordan, father of trailblazing educator Dock Jordan and father-in-law of Mary's brother, Morgan Hutchins. *Georgia Archives.*

91

following description of his environment in the prison system can be found in a report from 1944, just after the Georgia Department of Corrections was created:

> *An investigative committee from the General Assembly had visited county public works and State Highway Camps prior to the enactment of the new Correction Law and had officially reported to the Governor and the Assembly that many of the camps visited were filthy, unsanitary, poorly administered, and inadequately maintained and that in a number of them the prisoners were being treated brutally, and in some instances were being abused physically without cause. Under prevailing conditions in these camps, the term "Georgia Chain Gang" was no misnomer and along the county roads, as well as the principle highways of the state, prisoners garbed in the familiar convict stripes and fettered with archaic and torturous picks, leg irons, and other types of inhumane manacles, advertised the evils of the Georgia penal system to all passers-by.*

Even in the distaste of defeat, Ulysses was still driven to survive. He was not going to be content in those deplorable conditions. On October 15, 1935, nineteen years and two days after his initial conviction, Ulysses Goolsby escaped from the state highway camp near Powersville, Georgia. There is no date of recapture listed on his prison record.

EPILOGUE

As a researcher, I'm driven by my curiosity and my desire to learn as much as possible about a certain subject. Other genealogists will understand that this story was difficult to put together because of inaccuracies in some of the sources. Conflicting evidence is not uncommon at all, but there were some things that I truly couldn't resolve and decided to leave out of the story.

One of them is the identity of reported lynching victim James Burton. "Jim" was consistently listed as someone killed during the massacre, at the same time as Early Hightower. The problem is that there is no Black person with that name on the 1910 census in Early County, Georgia. After searching neighboring counties, I found two possibilities. One lived in Calhoun County, Georgia, and the other lived in Henry County, Alabama. Either could be the right person, but there is no accessible evidence that either moved to Early County before December 30, 1915. Each reported victim of the Early County Massacre either lived in the Urquhart district of the county or was a close relative of Grandison. Neither of the two Jims fit either category, but that still doesn't mean one of them isn't him.

When I began confirming who actually died in this incident, I started by looking at the 1920 census. The wives of Simon Goolsby, Grandison Goolsby and Edmond Law were all recorded as widowed in 1920, supporting the reports that those men were lynched. The Calhoun County Jim from 1910 seems to be the same as a "Jim Burden" living in Philadelphia during the 1920 census, based on his family unit and the birth location of his son. Even his existence in 1920 doesn't mean he isn't the Jim Burton from the newspapers in 1915. It was reported that a Black person was shot, but not fatally, which could've been Jim. Charlie Holmes and Charlie Givens were reported victims as well, but there are countless records proving that they survived.

Winget Harris, Grandison's brother-in-law, was also consistently named as a lynching victim, but he was very much alive, appearing on the 1920 census in Cleveland, Ohio. Several people related to this incident left Early County for the North, so it is definitely possible that the Philadelphia Jim is the right person. However, this period is a part of the Great Migration, and many Black Americans were moving north regardless of being connected to Grandison Goolsby. Winget is also a great example because his name was spelled wrong in each newspaper article. I spent years looking for "Wingate Harrison" before noticing Fredonia Goolsby married someone named Winget Harris. The same is true for Hash Jewell, another survivor, whose name was misspelled as Hosh and Josh in the media coverage. Winget and Hash's real names were George and Martin, respectively, adding another level of difficulty to discovering their identities. This goes to show that "James Burton" may be a misinterpretation of a real victim's name. If that's the case, this book is dedicated to the memory of that person as well.

Another unreconciled subject is the age of Grandison's sons. Ulysses testified under oath at his trial that he was born on March 14, 1898. Mike testified at his that he was born on July 13, 1900. I believe that they were both one year older than they claimed, and although it was common for people to forget when they were born, I'm not sure why they were mistaken about this. Birth certificates were not required yet, but the Goolsbys were from a community that generally kept track of their birth dates anyway. I take their birth dates from the 1900 census, which Mike wouldn't even have been in if he was born in July 1900.

The age statements in their testimonies could have been intended to evoke sympathy from the jury. I do admit that a seventeen-year-old and a fifteen-year-old would be looked at differently than an eighteen-year-old and a sixteen-year-old in current times, but I don't know if that was the case in 1916. The age of majority was twenty-one at that time, so I don't think subtracting a year to deceive the jury would have made a difference. Also, in the eyes of racist white people, Black boys as young as twelve have been considered a major threat worthy of execution. Ironically, those are the same people who continue to refer to us as boys well into our adulthood. It's also interesting that the age of majority was twenty-one, even though young girls were often married by the age of sixteen. Many of them already had three or four children by the time they were twenty-one.

I truly believe Ulysses and Mike were born in 1897 and 1899, and that won't change, but I was not there, so I can't say that I know for sure. However, I do have testimony from someone who essentially was there: Grandison's first cousin Girlie Harrison. She was recorded on video saying that she was fourteen days older than Ulysses. According to the 1900 census, Girlie was born in 1898, the year Ulysses also claimed at his trial. Even though she was about ninety years old in this recording, that is an odd thing to be mistaken about. She and Ulysses were first cousins, once removed. They were close and even lived on the same land for a period of time. Being born two weeks apart is something that would've been discussed regularly. This corroboration of Ulysses's younger age gives me pause, but I am still not convinced he was born in 1898, especially since Girlie's birthday was March 5. That isn't fourteen days from March 14 in any year, so she may have only remembered that the number fourteen was involved somehow and that they were close in age.

Another questionable detail involves some of the names in Ulysses's trial transcript. His testimony is the only evidence I have identifying the people who were with Ulysses when he was initially attacked by Henry Villepigue. Tobe Harris was recorded as T.B. Harris in the transcript, but there was no young Black person with those initials in Early County during that period. After looking at all the Harris families, I came to the conclusion that Ulysses was likely referring to Clem Harris, who was nicknamed "Tobe." Clem's brother Walter was married to Mattie Givens and therefore a brother-in-law to the other buggy passengers: Lillie Bell and Mollie Givens. The transcript says the four teenagers were all going to the wedding of Major Powell and Mollie Smith, but the bride's name was actually Leila Smith, so clearly there are some mistakes in it. The confusion could have stemmed from testimony about Mollie Givens. She was never referred to by name in the testimony, only as the sister of Lillie Bell Givens, so I discovered Mollie's name by looking at census records. Mollie Givens and Clem "Tobe" Harris were born in the same year.

As a general note, I excluded all oral history about the event that had been passed from those that were alive at that time, down to their children and grandchildren, and told to me over the phone or in writing. Their family stories were actually consistent but vastly different from what was reported in the *Early County News* and in the eyewitness statements. Most claimed that when the lynching mob found Grandison, he was hiding in a church steeple, not at Charlie Holmes's house. They also claimed that when Grandison began shooting at the mob, he killed several people. Some accounts say he killed nine people, while in Cissy Houston's book *How Sweet The Sound*, she wrote that he may have killed as many as fifty. Cissy's father was from Early County, and he told her the story.

Not one newspaper reported that any possemen died from Grandison Goolsby's bullets. Even Grandison's first cousin Girlie Harrison, who was physically present for some events, claimed that he killed several people. She was not an eyewitness to this, but she said that the white men ordered her and her family to not go anywhere near the scene of Charlie Holmes's house. She said that this was because they didn't want anyone to know how many white people he had killed. Cissy Houston also claimed that several folks were injured and had resulting amputations and that these people could be seen around town in the following years.

I don't want to discredit the information from these family members, but because none of them were actually there, I think they took what really happened and built around it. Ollen B. Hudspeth and Sam Pittman truly were shot by Grandison Goolsby that night. Sam did have an amputation because of the wound, and Ollen was shot in the head, so people may have assumed that he died. Furthermore, on January 3, 1916, it was reported on the front page of the *Greenville News* in South Carolina that a member of the lynching mob accidently shot himself in the leg while bragging about killing the Goolsbys in Blakely. He may have also been one of the injured men thought to have been shot by Grandison.

Morally, I'm grateful that I couldn't find documentation of Grandison killing all those people. I was already struggling with the idea of making Grandison the hero of this story because it first appeared as though he acted in revenge. This lynching was not as simple as a whistle or a false accusation of rape. Grandison and Ulysses shot and killed a white man in broad daylight. We will never know if Grandison intended to hurt Henry Villepigue on that fateful day, but I truly believe he wouldn't have brought his children with him if that was the case. Ulysses, Mike and Charlie Givens all testified that Henry Villepigue shot at Grandison first after expressing a desire to kill Ulysses. Everyone also testified that Grandison was very calm, didn't seem upset and that his guns were still concealed in the buggy when Henry started shooting. If that isn't justified homicide, I don't know what is. All secondary accounts of the "Grandison Goolsby War" portray Grandison as a murderer one way or another, but I am asserting that he was not. He defended his sons and protected their lives.

Even with all these inconsistencies, I am grateful for the opportunity to tell the story. The ancestors left me with so many pieces that were just waiting to be put together. I honor their memories and pray that their pain and suffering was not in vain. I share this information without fear, in hopes that we can stop these events from happening again.

ALPHABETICAL INDEX OF NOTABLE FIGURES

Surname	First Name	Life Dates	Significance
Atkinson	Samuel Carter	August 27, 1864–October 5, 1942	Georgia Supreme Court justice
Barksdale, MD	Cobb Rutherford	November 9, 1876–May 28, 1947	Trial witness
Beck	Marcus Wayland	April 28, 1860–January 21, 1943	Georgia Supreme Court justice
Bostick	Richard S.	1830–1858	Granduncle of Henry Villepigue
Bridges Sr.	John Oscar	January 25, 1881–March 20, 1952	Trial witness
Bridges	William Zachery Taylor	May 24, 1847–October 17, 1928	Father of John O. Bridges and Nettie Coachman
Castellow	Bryant Thomas	July 29, 1876–July 23, 1962	Pataula Judicial Circuit solicitor general
Castellow	Irene Villepigue	January 10, 1897–November 20, 1977	Wife of Henry Villepigue
Castellow	Robert Aubrey	July 27, 1889–December 26, 1951	Second husband of Irene Villepigue

Surname	First Name	Life Dates	Significance
Coachman	Edwin Horace	December 13, 1869–February 6, 1949	Employer of Henry Villepigue
Coachman	Herbert Lane	January 12, 1898–August 28, 1963	Buggy passenger of Henry Villepigue
Coachman	Mary Jeanette "Nettie"	July 10, 1876–November 10, 1960	Mother of Herbert Lane Coachman
Cohen	Mayer	September 10, 1883–January 12, 1942	Trial witness
Cornwell	Gibson Hill	April 25, 1867–June 8, 1936	Lawyer for Ulysses and Mike Goolsby
Davison	Robert Emmett	October 14, 1854–October 2, 1928	Prison commissioner
Dorsey	Hugh Manson	July 10, 1871–June 11, 1948	Governor of Georgia
Dumas	Hassel Sylvester	May 16, 1896–November 23, 1961	Buggy passenger of Henry Villepigue
Evans	Beverly Daniel	May 21, 1865–May 7, 1922	Georgia Supreme Court justice
Fish	William Hansell	May 12, 1849–December 8, 1926	Georgia Supreme Court justice
George	Walter Franklin	January 29, 1878–August 4, 1957	Georgia Supreme Court justice
Gilbert	Stirling Price	January 31, 1862–August 28, 1951	Georgia Supreme Court justice
Givens	Mollie	August 1899–unknown	Buggy passenger of Ulysses Goolsby
Givens	Willie Wiggins	January 1892–unknown	Wife of Charlie Givens

Surname	First Name	Life Dates	Significance
Givens Jr.	Charlie	April 15, 1889–August 6, 1927	Friend of Ulysses Goolsby
Goolsby	Alpheus "App"	1874–unknown	Son of Mike Goolsby and Sarah Law
Goolsby	Grandison R.	November 1869–December 30, 1915	Son of Mike Goolsby and Sarah Law
Goolsby	Julian Ransome	October 3, 1884–July 4, 1970	First husband of Charlotte Reynolds
Goolsby	Mary M. Hutchins	February 28, 1870–March 7, 1924	Daughter of Charles Hutchins and Analiza Brooks
Goolsby	Mike Atrus	July 13, 1899–October 18, 1940	Son of Grandison Goolsby and Mary Hutchins
Goolsby	Nathaniel Hawthorne	January 1, 1905–September 6, 1969	Son of Grandison Goolsby and Mary Hutchins
Goolsby	Roosevelt	October 29, 1901–February 5, 1972	Son of Grandison Goolsby and Mary Hutchins
Goolsby	Sarah	1848–1917	Daughter of Edmond Law Sr. and Hulda Law
Goolsby	Simon	October 1883–December 29, 1915	Son of Mike Goolsby and Sarah Law
Goolsby	Ulysses McKinley	March 14, 1897–unknown	Son of Grandison Goolsby and Mary Hutchins
Hall	Precious	June 1894–December 31, 1915	Adopted son of Edmond Law

Surname	First Name	Life Dates	Significance
Hamilton	Elvin Booth	February 4, 1888–April 2, 1931	Trial witness
Harris	Clem "Tobe"	June 3, 1899–September 15, 1982	Buggy passenger of Ulysses Goolsby
Harris	George Winget	April 1977–October 21, 1958	Brother-in-law of Grandison Goolsby
Harris	Nathaniel Edwin	January 21, 1846–September 21, 1929	Governor of Georgia
Henderson	Charlotte Reynolds	September 13, 1895–January 22, 1974	First wife of Julian Goolsby
Highsmith	James Parker	February 12, 1878–April 25, 1945	Superior Court judge
Hightower	Early	1880–December 30, 1915	Son of Preston Hightower and Delia Law
Hill	Hiram Warner	July 18, 1858–January 13, 1934	Georgia Supreme Court justice
Hines	James Kollock	November 18, 1852–March 19, 1932	Lawyer for Ulysses and Mike Goolsby
Hobbs	Lawton Carlyle	October 12, 1881–October 10, 1951	Blakely City marshal
Holmes	Charles	1865–November 22, 1952	Close friend of Grandison Goolsby
Holmes	Jacob	February 5, 1845–January 16, 1924	Father of Charlie Holmes
Howell	Robert Lee	January 4, 1866–July 13, 1953	Brother of Thomas Jackson Howell

Surname	First Name	Life Dates	Significance
Howell	Thomas Jackson	June 3, 1863–March 1, 1935	Early County sheriff
Hudspeth	Ollen Barbee	May 12, 1878–January 4, 1964	Member of lynching mob
Hutchins	Charles J.	May 1820–November 6, 1912	Father of Mary Goolsby
Hutchins	Charlotte Law	1863–August 22, 1946	Aunt of Grandison Goolsby
Jewell	Edward "Eddie"	November 23, 1891–December 10, 1957	Friend of Grandison Goolsby
Jewell	Martin "Hash"	March 1870–April 11, 1937	Friend of Grandison Goolsby
Law Jr.	Edmond	1847–December 31, 1915	Uncle of Grandison Goolsby
Lumpkin II	Joseph Henry	September 3, 1856–September 6, 1916	Georgia Supreme Court justice
McCullough	Marion Mosby	April 16, 1868–January 23, 1943	Trial witness
Munday	William Chenault	June 27, 1876–June 24, 1934	Lawyer for Ulysses and Mike Goolsby
Patterson	Thomas Edwin	October 8, 1868–June 9, 1927	Prison commissioner
Pittman	Samuel Lee	March 22, 1887–February 7, 1955	Member of lynching mob
Rainey	Eugene Leigh	January 21, 1863–June 19, 1936	Prison commissioner
Reynolds	William M. "Billy"	October 8, 1866–September 29, 1936	Father of Charlotte Henderson

Surname	First Name	Life Dates	Significance
Sherman	Joseph Sydney	1868–August 16, 1936	Trial witness
Singletary	Andrew Jackson	October 30, 1849–March 18, 1917	Trial witness
Sirmons	Robert Toombs "Dick"	April 22, 1875–March 1, 1949	Neighbor of Charlie Holmes
Stevens	Mary E. Bostick	1831–unknown	Grandmother of Henry Villepigue
Villepigue	Caroline Stevens	March 5, 1855–November 13, 1927	Mother of Henry Villepigue
Villepigue	Henry J.	August 1876–December 29, 1915	Assailant
Williams	Lillie Bell Givens	January 1897–unknown	Buggy passenger of Ulysses Goolsby
Worrill	William Charles	December 6, 1854–June 1, 1923	Superior Court judge

TIMELINE OF THE EARLY COUNTY MASSACRE

Date	Time	Address	Location	Event	Source
Tuesday, 12/28/15	Afternoon	Howard Landing Road	Five hundred yards east of Oak Grove AME Church	Henry Villepigue physically assaults Ulysses Goolsby	Trial transcript
Tuesday, 12/28/15	Around sunset	Gilbert Landing Road	Grandison Goolsby's house	Ulysses tells his mother what happened	Trial transcript
Tuesday, 12/28/15	Late at night	Old River Road	Charlotte Law's house	Grandison's mother tells him what happened	Girlie Harrison interview
Wednesday, 12/29/15	8:00 or 9:00 a.m.	Cuthbert Street	Andrew Jackson Singletary's store in Blakely	Grandison speaks with Andrew Singletary in front of his store	Trial transcript
Wednesday, 12/29/15	Between 10:00 and 11:00 a.m.	Cuthbert Street	Elvin Booth Hamilton's hardware store	Grandison goes in the hardware store	Trial transcript

Date	Time	Address	Location	Event	Source
Wednesday, 12/29/15	Noon	River Street	Joseph Sydney Sherman's house	Grandison speaks to Joseph Sherman for twenty or thirty minutes	Trial transcript
Wednesday, 12/29/15	1:30 p.m.	Howard Landing Road	Charlie Givens's house	Charlie Givens agrees to show Grandison the way to Henry Villepigue's house	Trial transcript
Wednesday, 12/29/15	3:00 p.m.	Chattahoochee River	Coachman Plantation	Henry Villepigue attempts to kill the Goolsbys and is fatally wounded	Trial transcript
Wednesday, 12/29/15	Evening	Cedar Springs	Hudspeth Plantation	Hash and Eddie Jewell arrive at Ed Law's house with Ulysses and Mike	Grand jury indictment
Wednesday, 12/29/15	Late at night	Old River Road	Goolsby Plantation	Simon Goolsby lynched by mobs	*Early County News,* 1/6/16
Wednesday, 12/29/15	Late at night	Cedar Springs Road	Atlantic Coast Line Saffold depot	Ed Law and Precious Hall put Ulysses and Mike on the westbound night train	Grand jury indictment

Timeline of the Early County Massacre

Date	Time	Address	Location	Event	Source
Thursday, 12/30/15	Morning	Old River Road	Early Hightower's cabin	Early Hightower lynched by mobs	*Early County News*, 12/30/15
Thursday, 12/30/15	Early afternoon	Old River Road	Pleasant Grove	Supreme Circle Lodge burned by mobs	*Early County News*, 1/6/16
Thursday, 12/30/15	Late afternoon	Union Road (formerly called Rock Hill Road)	Charlie Holmes's farm	Grandison is lynched while fleeing from Charlie Holmes's burning house	*Early County News*, 1/6/16
Thursday, 12/30/15	Night	North Church Street	Starlight Masonic Lodge and Grand United Order of Odd Fellows Lodge	Lodges burned by mobs	*Early County News*, 1/6/16
Friday, 12/31/15	About 1:00 p.m.	Cedar Springs	Hudspeth Plantation	Mobs lynch Edmond Law Jr. and Precious Hall for helping Ulysses and Mike Goolsby escape	*Early County News*, 1/6/16
Friday, 12/31/15	Night	Hilton	Zion Watch Lodge No. 285, Prince Hall Free and Accepted Masons	Lodge burned by mobs	*Early County News*, 1/6/16

TIMELINE OF *THE STATE VS. GOOLSBY*

January 3, 1916	Sheriff Thomas Jackson Howell requests arrest warrant for Charlie Givens and Judge Thomas Jackson Lanier signs it
January 10, 1916	Policeman Henry Thomas King requests arrest warrant for Ulysses Goolsby and Judge Thomas Jackson Lanier signs it
January 19, 1916	Mary Goolsby sells her plantation, likely for funds to retain lawyers for her sons
January 21, 1916	City marshal Lawton Carlyle Hobbs goes to Mississippi to investigate suspicious letter
January 26, 1916	Sheriff Thomas Jackson Howell arrests Ulysses and Mike Goolsby in Cleveland, Mississippi
March 20, 1916	Subpoenas issued for prosecution witnesses Charlie Givens and Mike Goolsby to testify for the grand jury

April 12, 1916	Hearing on a motion for change of venue, which is denied by Judge William Charles Worrill, and defense counsel appeals
June 27, 1916	Supreme Court of Georgia evenly divided on the appeal, which affirms Judge Worrill's decision
October 13, 1916	Ulysses Goolsby is tried and convicted of first-degree murder
October 14, 1916	Mike Goolsby is tried and convicted of second-degree murder
October 14, 1916	Ulysses Goolsby is sentenced to death and Mike Goolsby is sentenced to life in prison
October 14, 1916	Defense counsel makes a motion for a new trial
December 30, 1916	Hearing on a motion for a new trial, which is denied by Judge William Charles Worrill, and defense counsel appeals
January 1, 1917	Ulysses Goolsby is deposed at the clerk's office to say that he is out of legal funds
February 27, 1917	Morgan Hutchins mortgages his farm, possibly for funds to maintain legal representation for his nephews
July 11, 1917	Supreme Court of Georgia hears motion and grants Mike Goolsby a new trial
August 31, 1917	Supreme Court of Georgia hears motion and grants Ulysses Goolsby a new trial
October 8, 1917	Second set of trials is postponed due to Judge Worrill's illness
December 11, 1917	Judge James Parker Highsmith presides over the trials and acquits Mike Goolsby

December 13, 1917	The jury returns a guilty verdict for Ulysses and his counsel moves for a new trial
February 23, 1918	Hearing on a motion for a new trial, which is denied by James Parker Highsmith, and defense counsel appeals
October 16, 1918	Supreme Court of Georgia grants Ulysses Goolsby a new trial
April 15, 1919	Ulysses Goolsby is tried and convicted of first-degree murder
April 17, 1919	Ulysses Goolsby is sentenced to death and his counsel moves for a new trial
June 21, 1919	Hearing on a motion for a new trial, which is denied by Judge William Charles Worrill, and defense counsel appeals
March 9, 1920	Supreme Court of Georgia denies the motion for new trial and affirms Judge Worrill's ruling
April 9, 1920	Ulysses Goolsby is resentenced to death

LANDHOLDINGS OF GRANDISON AND MARY GOOLSBY IN EARLY COUNTY

District	Land Lot	Acres	Description	Cost
28	184	25	off the southwest corner	$25
28	167	0.62	bounded by Colored Academy, Mrs. R.W. Davis and Church Street	$200
28	284	100	off south half	$125
5	340	150	whole lot except southwest and southeast corners	$750
5	302	123	entire west half	$800
28	166	0	Town Lots 70, 71, 72, 73, 74, on the west side of Church Street	$125
5	339	100	off the east side	$700
28	166	0	Town Lot 53, on the west side of Church Street and fronting Andrew Street	$1
5	338	124	whole lot except land sold to E.B. Hudspeth, Pleasant Grove Churches, Crumbley, and Mary Goolsby	$200
5	338	25	commencing where white church land crosses road, then east to Hudspeth line, then along Hudspeth line to land lot line, then north enough make 25 acres when crossed to River Road and down to starting point	$300
5	298	50	off the south side	$930
5	298	0.18	25 yards on two sides and 35 on the other two	$15

Grantor	Grantee	Date	Book	Page	Recorded
John Washington Franklin Webb	Grandison Goolsby	February 1, 1896	T	215	February 4, 1896
John Washington Franklin Webb	Grandison Goolsby	August 23, 1896	T	309	September 11, 1896
John Washington Franklin Webb	Grandison Goolsby	August 27, 1896	T	309	September 11, 1896
Thomas Temples	Mary Goolsby	October 15, 1904	W	577	October 18, 1904
Andrew J. and Luther Singletary	Mary Goolsby	December 14, 1908	25	495	February 1, 1909
Andrew Jackson Ross	Mary Goolsby	April 23, 1910	30	53	September 9, 1915
First National Bank	Mary Goolsby	November 3, 1910	26	558	November 3, 1910
Andrew Jackson Ross	Mary Goolsby	July 8, 1911	30	54	September 9, 1915
Andrew J. Singletary	Mary Goolsby	January 24, 1912	28	254	February 2, 1912
Andrew J. Singletary	Mary Goolsby	January 24, 1912	28	255	February 2, 1912
Mary's siblings	Mary Goolsby	February 10, 1913	28	401	March 6, 1913
Charlie B. Hutchins	Mary Goolsby	May 6, 1913	30	18	March 16, 1915

BLACK FRATERNAL ORGANIZATIONS IN EARLY COUNTY

G randison Goolsby was an active member of several Black fraternal orders in Early County. He was the Most Honorable Ruler of the Supreme Circle of Benevolence, an organization started by Henry S. Davis in Albany, Georgia. My ancestor Francis Terrell Hanks was likely a charter member soon after its founding in 1898, since they paid for her headstone in 1902. She may have been a member of Grandison's lodge near Pleasant Grove, where her father, Albert Terrell, was a prominent figure decades earlier. Francis is buried in Clay County, Georgia, at Mount Calvary Cemetery. Another Supreme Circle headstone can be found in the same cemetery, belonging to Moses Johnson. Moses was born enslaved on the Robert Yelldell Plantation, just like Grandison's mother.

Most notably, Grandison was the Worshipful Master of Starlight Lodge No. 95, the Blakely chapter of Prince Hall Free and Accepted Masons. The Grand Historian of the Most Worshipful Grand Lodge of Georgia shared with me that Grandison's lodge was chartered on June 25, 1891. I later discovered the deed for the lodge's town lot, which was purchased for fifty dollars on December 13, 1893, from founding member Joy Moses. He purchased a quarter acre earlier that year from Black women in the Society of the Grand United Hope of America. Then, he deeded a quarter of that quarter acre to Chappell Fairfax, Worshipful Master, and Jacob Holmes, Treasurer.

The Grand Historian also sent me membership lists from 1891, 1896 and 1912, providing valuable context for researching the Black leaders of

Early County. The lists are transcribed here in this chapter. Unfortunately, I recognized the first name on the list, as Sidney Grist was another lynched family member of mine.

It seems as though Grandison was not the only powerful Black man killed extrajudicially in this area. Sidney was also a trustee of the Colored School of Blakely, adjacent to Wesley Chapel AME Church, according to a deed dated January 30, 1890. Starlight Lodge founding member J.W.F. Webb deeded land to Sidney and other trustees such as Allen Robinson, Wesley Hansom, Benjamin Shoemake, Seaborn Perry, Charley King, John Ridley, Elijah Hodges, John Cain and Jackson Adams. Starlight Lodge and Grandison Goolsby's Blakely land were all in the same land lot as the school.

STARLIGHT LODGE No. 95—1891

Sidney G. Grist, Worshipful Master
Edmond Dawson, Senior Warden
J.A. Holmes, Junior Warden
H.S. Harris, Treasurer
John Washington Franklin Webb, Secretary
G.W.M. Mosley, Senior Deacon
Grandison R. Goolsby, Junior Deacon
Lawson Hartwell Hunter, Steward
C.B. Brown, Steward
W.A. Pierce, Chaplain
G.W. Bowen, Marshal
A.S. Ramsbor, Tyler
J.C. Moore
J.D. Frank
B.J. Frank
Joy Moses
J.W. Porter
Green M. Mosley

STARLIGHT LODGE NO. 95—1896

Harris Chappell Fairfax, Worshipful Master
Jacob Holmes, Senior Warden
William Redding, Junior Warden
Sidney Grist, Treasurer
Richard H. Whitely, Secretary
William Mosely, Senior Deacon
Grandison R. Goolsby, Junior Deacon
Lawson Hartwell Hunter, Steward
Olden George, Steward
A.P. Powell, Chaplain
Jacob Moore, Marshal
Alex Page, Tyler

STARLIGHT LODGE NO. 95—1912

Grandison R. Goolsby, Worshipful Master
S.L. Montgomery, Senior Warden
Walter Theodore Hanson, Junior Warden
Jacob Holmes, Treasurer
George Winget Harris, Secretary
William M. Glenn, Senior Deacon
Ed Hutchins, Junior Deacon
Jacob Holmes, Senior Steward
M.S. Smith, Junior Steward
Andrew Freeman, Chaplain
Simon Peter Smith, Marshal
Alexander Page, Tyler
John McSimmons
William Redding
Monroe Ransom
William Low
Walter H. Glenn
W.J. Sanders
Abe Lemons
A.B. Bable

C.B. Brown
J. Jenkins
C. Anthony
C. Sanders
C.C. Chapman
C.C. Cranch
Oliver Mitchell Hutchins
H. Hutcherson
H.G. Keener
L.J. Scott
J.R. Griggs
Allen Grice Sr.
Emanuel Ragland
Darius R. Holmes
Charles Holmes
Thomas Miles Goolsby
M. Cowing
C.H. Nickerson
C.E. Latimore
W.M. Weaver
Idus Tull
Isaac Foster
M.J. Monger
A.P. Powell
J.G. Goolsby
J. Glenn
H.S. Harris
J.H. Shaw
L.C. Cooper
Green M. Mosley
D. Adams
W.E. Moses
C. Crap
S.M. Williams
C.H. Latimore
Major John Powell
Albert Tull
Harris Chappell Fairfax

SID GRIST MURDERED NEAR BLAKELY, GA.

Was a Politician and a Hater of White Men — His Death Causes No Surprise in Neighborhood.

Special to The Journal.

BLAKELY, Jan. 2.—The particulars of a tragedy in this county two nights ago have just been learned here.

In the early part of the night unknown parties rode up to the house of Sid Grist, a notorious negro, and called him out. As he opened the door five Winchester bullets were fired into his body, killing him instantly.

Grist lived several miles from here on the Blakely and Arlington road. He was a notorious politician and hater of white men. It has been expected for a long time that some one would kill him, and little surprise was occasioned by the news that he had been so dealt with.

The *Atlanta Journal*, January 2, 1897.

The Killing of Sidney Grist.

BLAKELY, January ...

To the Editor of The Journal:

We, the undersigned citizens of Early county, having read in the Saturday Journal a special from this place, giving an account of the killing of Sidney Grist, near this town, wish to disabuse the mind of the public that he was a "notorious character," "a white man hater," and that it has been for a long time expected that he would be killed.

We have known Sidney Grist for a number of years, while it is true he has ever been a staunch Republican, and has worked hard for the Republican candidates, he did it in such way as to offend no one. He has always been courteous and respectful in his manner to the white men. He was a consistent member of the church and did much to encourage the elevation of his race.

The killing of Sidney Grist was not expected. The people of Early regret it very much.

G. D. Oliver, mayor of Blakely; J. H. Hand, M. D.; Geo. E. Christead, T. C.; C. E. Black, sheriff of Early county; P. D. DuBose, attorney at law; J. W. Alexander, councilman; J. W. Strickland, treasurer of Early county; R. Perryman, Ordinary of Early county; C. E. Stuckey, marshal; J. M. Nahler, T. J. Jones, policeman; Arthur Gray Powell, county judge; Thos. Williams, ex-county judge of Early county; R. W. Davis, member of board of education; T. M. Howard, editor Early County News; J. T. Freeman, clerk of superior court; J. J. Smith, H. C. Fryer, postmaster; J. B. Livingston, express agent; A. M. Irwin, N. P. & Ex J. P.

The *Atlanta Journal*, January 6, 1897.

REFERENCE LIST

The State of Georgia v. Ulysses Goolsby
The State of Georgia v. Mike Goolsby

Georgia Reports:
Goolsby v. State, 145 Ga. 424 (1916)
Goolsby v. State, 147 Ga. 169 (1917)
Goolsby v. State, 147 Ga. 259 (1917)
Goolsby v. State, 148 Ga. 474 (1918)
Goolsby v. State, 150 Ga. 66 (1920)

Early County News. November 20, 1902.
———. April 13, 1905.
———. June 8, 1911.
———. December 30, 1915.
———. January 6, 1916.
———. January 20, 1916.
———. January 27, 1916.
———. February 17, 1916.
———. April 13, 1916.
———. June 29, 1916.
———. July 13, 1916.
———. October 12, 1916.
———. October 19, 1916.

————. December 21, 1916.
————. September 6, 1917.
————. October 11, 1917.
————. December 13, 1917.
————. December 20, 1917.
————. April 17, 1919.
————. March 11, 1920.
————. April 1, 1920.
————. April 15, 1920.
————. May 6, 1920.
————. June 3, 1920.
————. July 22, 1920.
————. August 19, 1920.
————. September 2, 1920.
————. September 16, 1920.
————. September 23, 1920.

Georgia, State Board of Corrections:
Annual report the State Department of Corrections for fiscal year 1943–44.

UNEDITED TRANSCRIPTIONS
OF COURT RECORDS

Briefs of the evidence in both Ulysses and Mike's trials exist in the Early County Courthouse in Blakely, Georgia. The documents are typewritten and folded up within motions for new trials. Many names are spelled differently than the spellings that are considered correct today, and those spellings have not been changed within this unedited transcription. Interestingly, the contraction *wasn't* is almost exclusively spelled "want" or "wont." The transcripts don't include any questions or objections from the prosecutor or defense attorneys or statements from the judge, which were not included in the brief. They contain only witness responses, formulated in complete sentences. The transcripts include testimony from the following witnesses:

The State v. Ulysses Goolsby

1. Charlie Givens
2. Irene Villepigue
3. Marion Mosby McCullough
4. John Oscar Bridges
5. Mayer Cohen
6. Dr. Cobb Rutherford Barksdale
7. Elvin Booth Hamilton
8. Joseph Sydney Sherman
9. Ulysses Goolsby

The State v. Mike Goolsby

1. Andrew Jackson Singletary
2. William Drayton Odum
3. Dr. Felix Patrick Davis
4. Joseph Sydney Sherman
5. Edwin Horace Coachman
6. Thomas Jackson Howell Sr.
7. Joseph Sydney Sherman (recalled)
8. Elvin Booth Hamilton
9. Charles Givens
10. Irene Villepigue
11. Marion Mosby McCullough
12. John Oscar Bridges
13. Mayer Cohen
14. Dr. Cobb Rutherford Barksdale
15. Thomas Jackson Howell Sr. (second statement)
16. Mike Goolsby

Virtually, both trials had the same witnesses that testified generally about the same things. There are minor differences noticeable in the testimonies that survive from both trials. In addition to the consistent name misspellings, there are minor typos that have also been included in the following transcription.

The State of Georgia vs. Ulysses Goolsby, et al.

Indictment for Murder

Early Superior Court, October Term, 1916.
Verdict of Guilty and Sentence.
Motion for new trial.
Ulysses Goolsby being tried alone.

--BRIEF OF THE EVIDENCE:--

Charlie Givens, sworn in behalf of the State, testified:
My name is Charlie Givens. I know the defendant in this case, Ulysses Goolsby. He is present in Court, the one on the right there, the one sitting next to the white man, the one with blue trousers on

(indicating). I do not know how old a man Ulysses Goolsby is. I've known him about three or four years. I knew H.J. Villipigue in his lifetime. He is dead. He was killed. I was present at the time H.J. Villipigue was killed. It was in Early county. He was killed with a breach-loaded shot gun and a rifle. He was killed with this last gone Christmas, during Christmas week. I knew Granderson Goolsby. He was the father of Ulysses Goolsby and Mike Goolsby. I saw Granderson Goolsby, Mike Goolsby, and Ulysses Goolsby on the day H.J. Villipigue was killed. This was before H.J. Villipigue was killed. The first time I saw them that day they stopped in front of my house. Me and my wife staid there together. My father did not live there. My father staid at the next house, about three hundred yards from my house. Then Granderson Goolsby and his two boys, Ulysses and Mike, stopped in front of my house, my father was at my home. My father is about fifty-four years old. I am twenty-seven years old. At this time, Granderson Goolsby and his two boys were traveling in a buggy. They were driving a mule. Granderson Goolsby was driving. One of the boys was sitting on the right hand side of the buggy and the other boy was sitting in the middle. Mike Goolsby was sitting in the middle. When they came up to my house they were going towards Mr. Villipigue's house. Granderson Goolsby lived about four miles from my house, back northeast from our house. Ulysses Goolsby and Mike Goolsby lived with Granderson Goolsby. In going from Granderson Goolsby's home to H.J. Villipigue's home, they would have to come by my house. It is the nearest way. It is about two miles from my house to Mr. Villipigue's house, two miles west from where I live. That makes the distance from Granderson Goolsby's home to Mr. Villipigue's home about six or seven miles. It was about one-thirty or two o'clock in the evening when Granderson Goolsby drove up in front of my house. When they drove up in front of my house they stopped, neither of them got out of the buggy. I was in the house when they drove up. My father and I were sitting by the fire in our house talking. Granderson Goolsby called for my father and I went to the door and he asked if my father was there and I told him yes. Ulysses and Mike were in the buggy at that time. Granderson Goolsby asked me if my father was there. He told me to tell my father to step out there and my father get up and went out there and he asked my father to come and go and show him the way to Mr. Villipigue's house, that he wanted to go there and see him, he said him and his boy had got in a fuss and he wanted to go and see if he could straighten it out, and my father told him he did not feel like going, and he asked me if I would go, and I told him I would go, and I went to the lot and caught my mule and rode the mule on down there behind them to Mr. Villipigue's house. I rode behind them. I was going to show them the way down to Mr. Villipigue's house. Neither Granderson Goolsby nor his boys said whether they knew the way or not, Granderson said he did not know the way and asked my father to come and show him the way, but my father said he did not feel like going and asked me if I would go. I did not see any weapon of any kind in the buggy at that time. It was a top buggy. The top was turned back. It was just leaning back, not pressed down. Neither one of them got out of the buggy at my house. I rode my mule behind the buggy they were in. Granderson Goolsby said he wanted to go to see Mr. Villipigue, and if his boy had damaged his team in any way he wanted to pay for it. I did not hear Ulysses Goolsby or Mike Goolsby say anything at all. That was all that was said between my father and Granderson Goolsby at my house. My father did not go, he staid at home. The road we were going did not go all the way to Mr. Villipigue's house; it goes by his house. It is a private road that goes down to the river. It passes in front of his house. Mr. Villipigue's house faces south. We were going west and the road let us in front of the house. The road is south of the house and the house faces the road. When we rode up to Mr. Villipigue's we stopped. I was behind Granderson Goolsby's buggy when it stopped. I was about five or six steps behind it. When the Goolsby buggy stopped, I stopped. Granderson was still driving. He was on the right hand side of the buggy. When the buggy drove up in front of the house and stopped, the buggy was facing west. When they drove up and stopped in front of Villipigue's house, that placed the mules head fronting towards the river. The buggy and mule did not remain in that position. When Granderson called Mr. Villipigue, he turned the buggy around. Granderson Goolsby called Mr. Villipigue as soon as he stopped. I did not see Mr. Villipigue before Granderson Goolsby called him, and I did not see anyone around his house. When Granderson drove up and stopped, he called Mr. Villipigue. He said, "Hello, Mr. Henry." No one answered. To the best of my knowledge, he called once. He called loud enough for them to hear him in the house. I did not hear anybody answer him. Mr. Villipigue came out of the house. When Granderson Goolsby called Mr. Villipigue, he was sitting in the buggy. When Granderson Goolsby hailed or called Mr. Villipigue, he turned around the buggy there. When he turned the buggy around, it was facing east, the direction we come from. It was in the direction of Granderson Goolsby's home. He did not get out of the buggy to turn it around. Both Mike and Ulysses Goolsby staid in the buggy when he turned it around. When he turned the buggy around, it was still in front of Mr. Villipigue's house. It was then about twenty yards from Mr. Villipigue's house. There was a fence around Mr. Villipigue's house and there was a gate immediately in front of his house. I do not know whether or not there is a hall to Mr. Villipigue's house. There is a porch to the house. The gate is about ten steps from the front door of the house. About that distance from the door steps. Granderson Goolsby was about ten steps from the gate. He turned the buggy around and stopped and Mr. Villipigue came out of the house then. I did not see any weapon in Mr. Villipigue's hand or anywhere about him as he come out of the house. I had not seen any weapon of any kind in the possession of either Granderson Goolsby, Ulysses Goolsby or Mike Goolsby up to that time. When Mr. Villipigue came out of the house, after Granderson Goolsby turned the buggy around, he got out of the buggy when Mr. Villipigue got in the yard. He got out on the right hand side of the buggy after he had turned around. After Granderson Goolsby got out of the buggy, he walked around the hind wheel, to the side that Ulysses Goolsby was sitting on and rested his hand in this position on the hind wheel. When Granderson got out of the buggy on the right, Ulysses Goolsby was sitting on the left and Mike between them. Granderson Goolsby got out on the right hand side and came around the back of the buggy to the left hand wheel and stopped on the front side of the back wheel. It put Ulysses Goolsby in hand reach of him. Then Granderson Goolsby got out of the buggy, Mike Goolsby did not change his position in the buggy. He was sitting on the seat, on the right side where his father had been sitting. Ulysses Goolsby remained on the left side of the buggy where he had been sitting. After Granderson Goolsby got to the left side of the buggy, Mr. Villipigue was about twelve yards from him, just coming on out, he stopped then. He kinder walked up west of the gate. Mr. Villipigue came out of the front gate. He kinder walked to the side like from Granderson Goolsby, on the west side of the buggy like, towards the mule's head east, kinder southeast. Mr. Villipigue got in about ten or twelve yards from Granderson Goolsby before he stopped. It was outside of the gate. Mr. Villipigue stopped and said, "Ain't that the boy I beat yesterday", and Granderson Goolsby said, "This is my son, and I brought him here to see if I could give you satisfaction", and Mr. Villipigue said, "No, look out I am going to kill him", and Granderson Goolsby said, "You kill me first" and wheeled back to get his gun and as he done that—He reached in front of his buggy, down in the foot of the buggy. I had not seen the gun up to that time. Granderson Goolsby pulled out a Winchester rifle from the foot of the buggy. It was pushed under the seat of the buggy and a sack spread over the stock—a croker sack, that would conceal it, I couldn't see it. I don't know exactly how long the gun was, something like about two feet; it was about that long. (Indicating.) About two feet or two and a half, about three feet, I reckon. Then Granderson pulled his rifle out from under the seat of the buggy, Mr. Villipigue shot a pistol. I do not know where he got the pistol from. When I first saw the pistol, it was in Mr. Villipigue's hand. When Mr. Villipigue first shot, Granderson was getting his rifle. Mr. Villipigue was about ten steps, I reckon, from Granderson Goolsby when he shot. Granderson pulled out his rifle and ran back away from Mr. Villipigue's gun. Granderson Goolsby got about three or four steps back further before he shot. This made them about fourteen feet apart. Granderson Goolsby shot at Mr. Villipigue. Mr. Villipigue shot the pistol three times, to my best recollection. I do not know whether Mr. Villipigue hit anybody or not. I did not hear Granderson Goolsby, Ulysses or Mike either claim to be hit. I did not see where either of them were wounded after that. I did not hear of either one of them complain of being wounded. Mr. Villipigue shot once before Granderson Goolsby shot his rifle, then Granderson Goolsby shot the rifle. After the rifle was shot, Mr. Villipigue shot once or twice. Granderson Goolsby then shot again. At Granderson's second shot, he struck Mr. Villipigue. I know he struck him, because Mr. Villipigue dropped his pistol down by his side. Mr. Villipigue's arm dropped to his side in which he held the pistol. After he dropped his hand to his side, Granderson shot once or twice more and Mr. Villipigue turned and started back to his house. He turned back facing the house. He went on to the gate and when he got to the front gate, he called his wife, and Ulysses shot at him with a shot-gun. Ulysses got the gun out from under the seat of the buggy. He got the shot gun from the same place where Granderson Goolsby got the rifle. It was a double barrell shot gun--a breech loader. It was under the seat in the buggy. Both rifle and gun were under the sack together. Neither were in the sack. When Ulysses got the gun from under the seat of the bugs, he shot at Mr. Villipigue when he was entering the gate going towards his house. Granderson was standing there with his rifle. Granderson had walked towards the buggy, kinder in the direction of Mr. Villipigue, as he was walking back towards the house. That would bring him closer to Mr. Villipigue, kinder in that direction. When Mr. Villipigue got to the gate going back to-wards the house, Ulysses got the gun from under the seat of the buggy and shot at Mr. Villipigue. Ulysses got out on the ground, he got the gun from under the seat of the buggy before he got out on the ground. He stepped out about two or three steps from between the wheels, when he stepped out two or three steps from the buggy wheels, he went in the direction of Mr. Villipigue's house, he then shot at Mr. Villipigue. At this time Mr. Villipigue was going towards the house. Mr. Villipigue was entering his gate and his back was to Ulysses. He was in that position when Ulysses shot. At the time Ulysses shot him with the gun, he was about ten yards from him. At the time Ulysses shot at Mr. Villipigue with the gun, I do not know exactly whether Mr. Villipigue had dropped his pistol or not, but he was going from Ulysses Goolsby. At that time, Mr. Villipigue was not endeavoring to shoot or hurt Mike, Granderson or Ulysses Goolsby. I do not know how many time Ulysses Goolsby shot at Mr. Villipigue with his gun, I know he shot once or twice. I do not know whether the load struck Mr. Villipigue or not. If Mr. Villipigue, fell, he fell in the yard. After Mr. Villipigue was shot at by Ulysses Goolsby, the last I saw of him he was going towards the house. Granderson Goolsby shot at him once more with his rifle after Ulysses Goolsby shot at him, when he was near his steps. Mr. Villipigue's back at the time Goolsby shot at him, was to Granderson, when Granderson shot at him with a rifle. At the time Granderson Goolsby shot at Mr. Villipigue with a rifle, Ulysses Goolsby had gotten back in the buggy and Granderson was standing on the ground by the buggy. I did not see Mr. Villipigue any more after Granderson shot at him with a rifle last. I was going back towards home then. I did not have an gun, rifle, pistol or anything. I did not stop until they got in the buggy and started. Granderson got in the buggy and started off and drove off about thirty-five yards and got out and went back and picked up his croker sack and I stopped and looked back then. That was back in front of Mr. Villipigue's house. That was the sack that the guns were under in the foot of the buggy under the seat. Granderson, Ulysses and Mike Goolsby got in the buggy and went on back home. I went on back home, too. I went behind them back home, I did not see Mr. Villipigue any more. This all occurred in Early County in December, 1915. I am no kin to Ulysses, Mike or Granderson Goolsby. I have no interest in this case.

--Cross:--

When we got to Mr. Villipigue's house, as soon as Granderson called him, he got up and came out of the house. Granderson called him "Mr. Henry". When Granderson drove up, he said, "Hello, Mr. Henry" and Mr. Villipigue came on out the house and when he returned out of the house, Granderson turned his buggy around, and after Mr. Villipigue got to the gate, Granderson gout out of the buggy and walked around to the side of the buggy where Ulysses Goolsby was. When Mr. Villipigue got near to him, about ten yards from him, he stopped and said, "Ain't that the boy I beat yesterday"; he was speaking about Ulysses, and Granderson said, "Yes, sir, that is my son, and I come to see if I can't give you some satisfaction", and Mr. Villipigue said, "No, look out I am going to kill him." When I noticed anything, when he said that, Granderson Goolsby turned to the buggy and got his rifle, and when I noticed, Mr. Villipigue had his pistol in his hand firing. Mr. Villipigue did not have his pistol when he said, "Look out. I am going to kill him." When Granderson got his rifle, Mr. Villipigue fired his pistol. Mr. Villipigue fired his pistol before Granderson got the gun. After he said, "Look out, I am going to kill him", he drew his pistol right at once, he got it while Granderson Goolsby was getting his rifle. Mr. Villipigue shot. I quit looking Mr. Villipigue's hand, when he said, "Look out, I am going to kill him". I quit looking at him when Granderson Goolsby was trying to get his rifle and I paid attention to him. I don't know where Mr. Villipigue got his pistol. He did not have it in his hand when he first got there, when he said "Look out", I don't know whether he had his pistol in his hand or not. I do not know how he was holding the pistol when he shot, he just shot. I cannot tell who he shot at. He just shot towards the buggy. Ulysses and Mike Goolsby were sitting in the buggy. Granderson was standing between the wheels of the buggy getting his rifle. When Mr. Villipigue said "Look out, I am going to kill him", nobody had said anything up to that time to indicate any trouble or any difficulty. Mr. Villipigue started it by saying "Look out, I am going to kill him", and drew his pistol and shot. When Mr. Villipigue shot, Granderson Goolsby ran back of the buggy and immediately shot. Granderson Goolsby did not have his gun when Mr. Villipigue shot, he didn't have it, but he was getting it. He was getting it when the first shot was fired. When Mr. Villipigue shot, Ulysses was sitting in the buggy by his brother. He wasn't doing anything at all. He had not said anything. I did not hear him say anything at all. All the shooting from the time the first shot was fired until it was over, was all done at once, in a very short time. I was considerably excited. My mule, when the first shot was made, jumped and threw me at the start. The mule hitched to Goolsby's buggy did not start off. I could have seen it. I do not know that the mule hitched to the buggy started to run away. and these boys in the buggy were trying to hold it. When the shooting started, I jumped off of my mule and got off out of the way. I ran off as soon as the trouble started. I know what took place, because I was where I could see. About twenty yards below. No, sir, I want any mile off. I got down off my mule when it first started. When Mr. Villipigue begun to shoot, my mule begun to jump and flounce, and when the first fire was made I jumped off the mule and led her out of the way. I got off out of the way, but I could see it. I could see them all right enough and see what was going on. I did not make any effort to go to the buggy and try to stop it. I was leading my mule along with me and when I stopped I was holding him, too. I got back on my mule after they passed by going on back home, after Granderson and his two boys passed. I followed them on back. They did not go into the yard that I know of. I don't know exactly how many times they shot, but I know who all shot. I know Mike Goolsby. He didn't do anything that I know of. I didn't see anybody else there. I did not see anybody else in the house, or around the house. I live about six miles west along the Howard and Landing road. I farm. I have been in jail the last six months, on this case. I don't know that there has been any charge made against me in this case. I have not been notified of any charge. Have just been in jail. I have been talking to nobody about this case. I have talked with Mr. Castello about it, and the sheriff, and that is all I have talked to.

MRS. IRENE VILLIPIGUE, sworn in behalf of the State, testified:

H.J. Villipigue was my husband. He is dead. He was killed. I was present when he was killed. I was at home on the day he was shot. I had been at home that day about two and one-half hours before the shooting. Mr. Villipigue brought me home. We reached home on that day about twelve-thirty o'clock in the afternoon. Just before the shooting, my husband was in the room with me. I do not remember when he left the room because I was asleep. The shooting waked me up. The shooting was in front of the house. From the house about twice as far from here to the wall of the court room back there, I guess. When I waked up, Mr. Villipigue called me to carry him the shot gun. I got up and carried the gun to the front door of our house. There was a hall and front porch to the house. I did not get any further than the front door of the house. When I got to the front door, I could see what was going on in front of the house. I saw three negroes and my husband. One was sitting in a buggy. I could see only just one arm of him, they had the top turned so I could not see him. The other two were shooting. One was there that he pointed out as I was going home. I think the one there, with the blue overall suit on (pointing our Ulysses Goolsby). He was shooting with a pistol, I think. He had a gun and a pistol in his hand. Don't know which one he was shooting. The other man was shooting with a pistol. My husband was coming towards the house. I never saw a weapon in his hand. I did not see my husband with any weapon at all. He was walking towards the house right from them with his back to them. He never turned in the direction of them. Do not know how many shots were fired by the negroes. Did not see my husband do any shooting. My husband fell in the hall. I was standing by his side when he fell. He lived just a few minutes after he fell. Don't know how many shots were fired by the parties. After my husband fell in the hall, the negroes went off a little piece, turned around and came back towards the house and left again. I did not see any pistol in the yard or about the yard or in the hall after they left. I do not know that my husband had a pistol when he came into the hall by me. I did not see any pistol shoot only in the way I have described.

--Cross Examined:--

I was asleep at first and was waked up by the shooting. Was in my room at that time. My room was about as far as from here to the wall. All the shots were fired kinder rapidly, pretty much together. Ulysses Goolsby had a pistol and a gun. I saw the pistol and gun. I can't tell how long the pistol was. He had it in his hand, held it up shooting. He had the gun in his hand. Both of them did not have their hands that way. I don't know which one it was. It might have been the old man so far as I know. I don't know how long the gun was the man had. I saw the gun. They had them in their hands holding them in their hands this way (Indicating,) but the one that was doing the shooting with the pistol this way, had his gun in his hand holding it down by the side of him. Am not positive which one it was. It was about three o'clock in the afternoon. I was asleep in the bed when my husband called for the gun. The shooting was taking place. It did not stop when he first called. It had not stopped when I got to the door. Was asleep when I heard the shooting take place in rapid succession. The door was not open. I opened the door. When I got to the door, they were still shooting, I did not come any further than the door. Could not tell how many shots were fired. When I woke up, my husband was calling me to bring his gun. I saw three negroes. I did not see but three.

M. M. McCullough, sworn in behalf of the State, testified:

I knew H.J. Villipigue in his lifetime. I knew him as Henry Villipigue. I was right near his home at the time he was shot. I saw four men come up just before the shooting took place. They were coming from the east going west towards Mr. Villipigue's house. I was going south in the edge of the swamp, hauling some cord-wood. I did not know any of the parties, but I knew the mule and I stopped the wagon. I could not swear that I heard the shooting, but I thought I did, and I stopped the wagon, but I did not hear any report of any shooting and the stockade was between me and the house where the shooting was. I could not say it was a pistol I heard shoot or not, there was a loose plank in the carry-log on the wagon and it kept rattling, and I couldn't say whether it was a gun I heard shoot or not, but I thought I heard some one shooting and I stopped the wagon, but I did not hear it again. After the parties came in there, I knew in about, I suppose, five minutes that there had been trouble at the house. Mrs. Villipigue sent a negro after me, I don't know the boy's name. He was from Alabama. I went right to Mr. Villipigue, when I got to the house, he was lying in the hall of his house, in the northend of the hall. The hall was about sixteen feet long, and he had walked in the front door, on the south, and walked through the hall and fell in the hall with his head in the corner at the north end of the hall. When I got to Mr. Villipigue, he was dead. Before Mrs. Villipigue sent for me, the mule that was hitched to the buggy came running down the fence and the one that was one the mule run and caught the mule that was hitched to the buggy, and stopped, three more men looked to be the same ones, went and got in the buggy and went driving back east, the way they had come. I did not recognize either one of them at that time. When I got to Mr. Villipigue, he was dead. I did not observe any wounds on his body, only one in his right side. I was there when Mr. Villipigue was undressed and dressed for burial, but I was not in the room. I only picked him up off the floor and carried him and laid him on the bed. I am no kin to Mr. Villipigue or his wife. At that time, I was hauling cord-wood for him.

J.O. BRIDGES, sworn on behalf of the State, testified:

I knew H.J. Villipigue in his lifetime. I saw him after he was shot and dead. I saw him out where he was killed, out at his home. I saw his body on the bed. I helped dress him and examined his body. I saw his body after his clothes were stripped from it. Observed wounds on his body. One ball went in right along there in his right arm, just below the elbow. I would judge it to be a pistol or rifle ball wound, and the ball lodged under the skin, just above the joint of the elbow, at the back of the arm, about two and a half or three inches above the elbow, it fractured a bone. All the balance of the wounds were on the back, there was a big hole right under the right shoulder blade. It ranged diagonally through the body, and bulged his left nipple out. It was a big hole. You could put your thumb in the place where it entered. I have had experience in firearms. The wound I have just described I would judge that it was inflicted by a cut shell. To make a cutshell, you take a shot-gun shell loaded and you cut around the hull part of the shell, right where the shot and the powder join, and when the explosion occurs that blows off the whole thing where it is cut around and the shell goes in a solid body. I would say in my best judgment, from the observation of that wound, and my knowledge of the effect of a cut shell, that the wound I have described going in under the right shoulder shoulder blade was caused from a cut shell fired from a shot gun. In my best judgment, I would think that the shot was fired from a pretty close range. Of course, I cannot give anything accurate as to distance. A cut shell will carry the shot in a wad further than an uncut shell will carry the shot in a wad. Say, take a shell that is not cut out around and shoot it out of a shot gun from here to that door there, the shot would scatter, but you take a cut shell and shoot it that distance, and the shot would make a hole in a wad. It is about fifty or sixty feet to the back of that wall. There was a wound upon the head of Mr. Villipigue. A pistol or rifle ball that went in just to the right of the center of the head in the rear, and went through and lodged over the left eye, you could feel the ball through the skin on the left eye. There was another would, I would judge had been fired from a shot gun loaded with buck shot, and that cut this right ear and went into the temple a little bit. I would judge that the shot was fired at an angle of sixty degrees on the right of Mr. Villipigue from the rear. My recollection is, there were six or seven holes in his body from his knees to his neck that were fired from a rifle or made with buckshot, the buckshot made a hole about the size of a thirty-two pistol ball. They entered from the back a little to the right of a direct line in the rear. one shot struck behind his right leg and came across his left leg, and I would judge from that that he was walking and the shot struck him on the right leg and came on and struck him on the left leg, as he was walking along, struck this part of his inside leg. No part of the wounds I have described could have been made from the front, except the one under his right arm. I am no kin to Mr. Villipigue.

--Cross Examined:--

I have had some experience with fire arms. Have not had very many occasions to notice wounds inflicted by fire arms, I have seen several, though, before that. I think only two months before that I saw one, a man killed here on the square and ranging all along for the past eighteen or twenty years, I have seen shot gun wounds. Some guns would scatter more than others, an ordinary choke-board gun would scatter over a space, I suppose, of about two or possibly two and a half feet in diameter, from here to that book-case. I saw some of the balls that were taken out of the body. They were buckshot. One or two in the back part of the body that had gone through the bone. They were ordinary buckshot. Did not see any one of the small shot in the body. I mean, the load that went through, it did not come out of his side, but went diagonally through the body. The shot that did not go through were left in the body. Did not see any one of these shot. The wound in diameter under the shoulder, where it entered, was big enough to put your thumb in the hole. I did not see any other would or shot immediately there. I never saw a rifle make that big a hole. Saw none of the shot in there. No effort was made to get the shot out that lodged under the nipple.

M. COHEN, sworn in behalf of the State, testified:

I knew Villipigue in his lifetime. I saw his body after his death out at the house where he was killed. I assisted in dressing his body for burial. I saw his body after his clothes were stripped off of him. I observed the wounds on his body. The biggest one was right under the shoulder blade and went through at an angle and bulged out right there, it went in right about here on the back, and came through and bulged out the skin right at the left nipple on the front. None of the shot that made the wound came through. The wound I have described was pretty good size, you could run your thumb in the hole, and there was another would on the back of his head. It entered right in the back of the head. It did not got through the head. I do not know where that bullet stopped. There was another wound on the side of his head; it looked like it touched the ear and went in the temple right about here, on the right, where I placed my hand now is at the back of the ear and it struck the temple about there. There was a wound in his right arm, it entered just back of the elbow in front, but didn't come through, it was slanting just above the elbow, it looked like was inside, we could feel it; it was at the back of the elbow, it went in at the front and we could feel it here on the back of the elbow. A number of big shot went in the back of Mr. Villipigue's body. I do not know how many, but quite a few; they were so badly scattered, I didn't count them; there were possibly half a dozen, or more. I am no kin to Mr. Villipigue or his wife.

--Cross Examined:--

I have not had very much experience with fire arms. I cannot say positively what those wounds were made by on the body of Mr. Villipigue.

DR. C.R. BARKSDALE, sworn in behalf of the State, testified:

My profession is in the practice of medicine. Have been in the actual practice of medicine for sixteen years. I knew H.J. Villipigue in his lifetime. I saw his body at his home before he was dressed for burial. I did not see him prepared for burial. I did not see the clothing removed from him after he was shot. I examined the wounds upon his body. The first wound I found was in his right arm, the ball entered below his elbow and ranged back up the arm, the two bones in the lower part of the arm being broken, and the bullet ranged around above the elbow and that wound appeared to have been made with a rifle or pistol ball. And in the back under the right shoulder blade, there was a big hole and it looked like a big load of shot went in there, but that didn't come out, and there were several scattered buckshot in his back. I could put my thumb in the hole under the shoulder; that wound seem to have been made with a load, and the one in the arm seemed to have been with a rifle or pistol ball. The shot in the back were buckshot, and some five or six scattering shot. I did not notice a wound in the back of the head. I did not examine the back of his head. From my examination of the wounds on the body of H.J. Villipigue after his death, I would say that the cause of his death was the gun shot wound under the right shoulder in the back. This was the fatal shot. I am not interested in this case in any way.

--Cross Examination:--

I would say that the wound n the right side just under the shoulder blade produced death. The direction the ball took, after entering, looked like it was going through the body. Not sideways, kinder towards the front. It ranged from the back towards the front in about this way. I didn't know that the person who fired the shot wont standing immediately at his back then. The shot entered under the right shoulder blade in the back and the ball ranged toward the front. No, sir, it did not range exactly through the body from the rear; it went kinder across this way. What caused the wound looked like a gunshot wound, made with a load of shot. I saw some of the shot; looked to be good big shot. Those were in the back. I don't know muchabout the size of shot, but they were good big shot, about the size of what is commonly known as buckshot. I have examined a good many wounds. If a gun was shot, loaded with buckshot, at a body as far off as from here to the back side of this court house, shot from an ordinary shotgun, the area over which the shot would scatter on an average would depend largely upon the boreof the gun shot, and also upon whether the shell had been cut or rung. The ordinary shell not rung or cut, just an ordinary shell in the average gun, if shot at an object as far as from here to the back of this court room, how much space the shot would scatter over, I don't know; I suppose it would scatter a few inches that distance. Some of the shot were in the side and some were in his back.

E.B. HAMILTON, sworn in behalf of the State, testified:
    I knew Granderson Goolsby. I am engaged in the hardware businesshere in Blakely, on Cuthbert Street; was engaged in that business last December. I remember the day that H.J. Villipigue was said to have been killed. Granderson come to my place of business on that day. Two boys were with him. I could not identify them positively. They were colored boys. Those two parties here, I cannot say, they seem to be about the same size, but I could not say positively they are the same two that were with Granderson Goolsby on that day.

J.S. SHERMAN, sworn in behalf of the state, testified:
    I knew Granderson Goolsby. I do not know his two soons, Ulyses and Mike. In answer to your question to look at these two boys here and say whether or not I ever saw them before with Granderson Goolsby, I will say that I saw the two boys with him, but I cannot say whether those are the ones or not, one of them had a scar on his face at the time I saw and looked at him; I had a side view to him. After comming a little nearer to see if I can identify either one of them as being with Granderson Goolsby, I will say they had their backs to me at the time I was looking at them; in fact, I didn't think much about it at the time, because I was talking to Granderson. It was the day that Mr. Villipigue was killed.
                            (The evidence for the State here closed.)

--STATEMENT OF THE DEFENDANT:--

    Gentlemen of the jury, I take my stand this morning to make my statement concerning the charge to the best of my understanding and to the best of my ability. On the 28th day of December, 1915, I-, myself, was invited to an infair that was given by a gentleman by the name of Major Powell, who married Miss Mollie Smith on the 28th day of December in the same year. On the 28th day of December, my father let me go to the infair. Well, it rained all day, especially all the morning, but that evening it quit raining and my father decided to let me go. I goes to Oak Grove Church, which is, to my understanding, about four miles south of my home. At that place, I was to get with a girl by the name of Lilly Bell Givens, who was a daughter of Mrs. Charles Givens, living with her brother, Charles Givens, Jr. I goes to his house and it come up a rain and after the rain was over, me and this girl and her sister and another boy, who I met there by the name of T.B. Harris, we got in the buggy and started to the infair, going towards the river. In going to the infair, I met this gentleman, and there was a hill about five hundred yards from the church and in about fifty feet of the hill I got out of the road and stopped, because we could not meet on the hill, and on the right hand side where I stopped at there was a clay bank, as near as I can estimate it, about ten inches high. He got in fifty feet of me; he told me to get out of the road; I did not say anything, but only pulled my mule out of the road and the mule got up on the bank in the cotton patch, and this gentleman, Mr. Villipigue, drew his pistol on me and cursed me. He come on close to my buggy and got out of his buggy with a pistol in his hand and come to the back of the buggy and started to kill me, and two little boys with him said he would not kill me, and the gentleman said, "Give me my buggy whip", and he got his whip and come back to the side of the buggy, on the left hand side of the road where I was, and begun to whip me, with his pistol in his left hand. I did not say anything; I did not even raise my hand to hurt him, or to say quit or nothing. And while he was whipping me, I was driving a scarry mule, and I was trying to hold the mule and keep him from running. I kept holding the mule and he was whipping me, and with his whip he struck me in my face, and all on my left side. After he quit whipping me, I turned, and the rest of them had got out in the cotton patch about twenty feet and the girl with me had got out of the buggy, too. I then goes on to another hill and went in a house and got some turpentine and put on my face where he had cut it with the whip and made it bleed. I turned and goes back home. I goes back to Charlie Given's house, Junior, and they asked me what was the matter and I told them. After I carried the girl back to her home, I staid there about an hour and three-quarters, which made it near sundown, and I left to go home. I came on home and my mother was at home, but my father wont there, but my mother and two brothers were there. I took out the mule and put it in the lot and come on in the house and my mother asked me what was the matter with me and I told her; she commenced crying, and I told her how it happened. I goes and feeds the mule and the hogs and I come on in the house and lay down across the bed, and when my father come home that night, I did not know when he come, and the next morning he come in after feeding the mule and he was crying and he asked me what was the matter with me; he said that he had heard that somebody had whipped me and he asked me how it was and I told him. He said he was going down there to see him and ask him about it, and if I was wrong in the matter he was going to whip me. I told him there was no need of going, and told him how it was, and that I did not want to go because the man tried to kill me for nothing and I did not want to meet him any more, and my father said "You must go", and I told him there was no need of it, but he said I have to go with him and he made me go with him. So, after breakfast, he hitched up the mule to the buggy and took me and my brother in the buggy and come on up town here, and after getting to town he staid here while and talked to two or three men, but I did not know what he was doing, and he did not tell us what he was going to do. After that he goes on out to Charlie Givens' house and we stopped and both them come out to the buggy, and my father asked old man Givens to go with him to show him the way, my father said he did not want a crowd to go with him down there, that he did not want to kill or hurt him, that he just wanted to go down there to find out whether I was wrong in the matter, and if I was he would whip me about it, and he just wanted somebody to show him the way down there, that he did not know the way. Charlie Givens father said he did not feel like going, and Charlie Givens said he would go with him to show him the way. We goes on down there, and when we got there, my father hailed and said, "Hello, Mr. Henry", and he come to the door and opened it and said "What do you want", and my father said, "I want to talk to you a little". At that time, he had his pistol in his left hand pocket, and he come on out of the gate, and I was sitting on the left hand side of the buggy, facing west, and turned around, facing east, and that throwed me on the north side of the buggy. Mr. Villipigue come on out of the gate and he looked and saw the scar on my face where he had hit me, and he said, "Ain't that the negro that jammed me yesterday", and my father said, "This is my son, and I have come to talk to you about it", and he said, "Get out of the way, God damn you, I am going to kill him", and my father said, "Please don't kill him, he wont to blame about it, why did you hit him", and when my father said that, he (Villipigue) said, "Get out of the way, I am going to kill him", and my brother was sitting right side of me with his face in the same direction I was facing; he pulled out his pistol and shot at me three times, and the mule started to run, but father got his gun and shot him as he throwed his pistol to shoot father my father shot him. He run back in the house and called for his shot gun, and we were trying to hold out mule, and when he run to the house and called for his gun, his wife brought the gun to the door and we come on away. We come on back home; my father said, "Boys, I would like for you to go on off, because I am satisfied they will kill me", but he said, "You all go on off and stay until I can settle it if I can, but you all go on off and be good boys", and them were the last words he told us, because he knew they were going to kill him or hang him, or something of that kind, and we goes on off, and what else was done I don't know. That is all that I know about it; I have told you, to the best of my ability, how it was. I was born in 1898, the 14th day of March, and that would make me eighteen years of age the 14th day of this last gone March. At the time this difficulty occurred, I was only seventeen years old at that time, and my brother fifteen years old and this past July he was sixteen, and I am now eighteen years of age, and he is sixteen years old and we are, therefore, minors.

(The evidence in the case here closed on both sides.)

The State of Georgia vs. Mike Goolsby, et al.

Indictment for Murder

Early Superior Court, October Term, 1916.
Verdict of Guilty, with recommendation for mercy, and sentence.
Motion for new trial.
Mike Goolsby being tried alone.

--BRIEF OF THE EVIDENCE:--

A.J. SINGLETARRY, sworn in behalf of the State, testified:
  I knew Granderson Goolsby. He is dead. I know his two sons, Ulysses and Mike Goolsby. I remember the occasion when H.J. Villipigue was killed. I saw Granderson Goolsby the day following the day H.J. Villipigue was killed. I did not see him that I know of on the day that Mr. Villipigue was killed. It was the day after the killing that I saw him. His sons, Ulysses and Mike Goolsby, were with him in town, they come in early and came to my store about eight or

nine o'clock. I did not have any conversation with Mike Goolsby. I had no conversation with Granderson Goolsby or Ulysses Goolsby in the presence of Mike Goolsby. I heard no statement made by Granderson Goolsby or Ulysses Goolsby in the presence of Mike Goolsby. They were traveling in a buggy, I think they were driving a mule; I think it was a black mule. They were riding in a single buggy. I think it was an open buggy, I am not sure. Granderson Goolsby, at that time, lived about six or seven miles northwest of Blakely. I know Charles Givens, I know where he lived at that time. I am mistaken about it; it was on the day that Mr. Villipigue we killed, it was before the killing of Mr. Villipigue, I saw Granderson Goolsby and his two boys. Yes, sir, I made a mistake in my testimony a while ago; that it was after the killing I saw these parties; I got confused about it; it was on the day before Mr. Villipigue was killed that day. At that time Ulysses Goolsby and Mike Goolsby were living with their father, six or seven miles northwest of Blakely. Charlie Givens was living at that time about six miles southwest of Blakely. The Goolsbys and Charlie Givens lived on different roads. H.J. Villipigue lived at that time about nine miles from Blakely; in going from Blakely to H.J. Villipigue's house, where he lived at that time, it was not the most direct route to go by where Granderson Goolsby and Ulysses and Mike Goolsby lived. To go from Blakely to Mr. Villipigue's home, you would go by where Charlie Givens lived at that time It was the most direct route Charlie Givens lived about two and a half or three miles from Mr. Villipigue's home. I said it was the morning of the same day Mr. Villipigue was killed and before he was killed that I saw Granderson Goolsby and his two sons, Ulysses and Mike, here in town. It was in the morning about eight or nine o'clock, I would presume; they come to my store and Granderson Goolsby drove back behind the store and hitched his mule and the boys and Granderson come to where I was. I was in front of the store, and the boys walked out a little piece and took their stand, and their father come to me and he was saying something to me and I asked him - - When Granderson Goolsby spoked to me the boys were off somewhere about as far from here to that rail and they took their stand out there while Granderson Goolsby and I were talking. My conversation with Granderson Goolsby was in an ordinary tone of voice. I was hardly talking as loud as I am now; we were just talking in an ordinary tone; I might be talking a little louder now, on account of letting the jury hear me than I was talking to Granderson Goolsby. He and I were just talking in an ordinary tone of voice. There was nothing between me and Granderson Goolsby and where Mike and Ulysses were standing. We were in plain view and in sight of them. There was not any crowd or congregation of people about there. There was no noise or things of that kind to obstruct the hearing between us. I cannot say from my recollection of the tone of voice in which Granderson Goolsby and myself were talking and my knowledge of the position of Ulysses and Mike Goolsby, during that conversation, whether Mike Goolsby was in a position to hear the conversation between Granderson Goolsby and myself as it occurred. I did not see Granderson Goolsby and this defendant, Mike Goolsby, when they left town. I will state that I had no conversation with Mike Goolsby himself.

--Cross Examined:--

I had known this boy, Mike Goolsby, ever since he was big enough to come to town with his father. He is fifteen or sixteen years of age, or was at that time.

<u>W.D. ODUM</u>, sworn in behalf of the state, testified:

I know the defendant in this case, Mike Goolsby. I did not know H.J. Villipigue in his lifetime. I remember the occurrence that H.J. Villipigue was killed. I did not see the defendant, Mike Goolsby, on that day.

<u>DR. F.P. DAVIS</u>, sworn in behalf of the state, testified:

I do not know the defendant in this case, Mike Goolsby.

<u>J.S. SHERMAN</u>, sworn in behalf of the state, testified:

I did not know H.J. Villipigue in his lifetime. I knew Granderson Goolsby. I had known him, I think, about a year before this difficulty. I knew him only since I had been in Blakely, in 1915. I remember the day that H. J. Villipigue was killed. I saw Granderson Goolsby in Blakely on that day. I think it was a few minutes after twelve o'clock. I had started to dinner, but stopped at my gate. I live in the western part of Blakely, on River street. Granderson Goolsby lived at that time out on the Ft. Gaines road; that is the road he went home. It was the most direct road to Granderson Goolsby's home from Blakely. The street I live on is not is not the most direct way to Granderson Goolsby home from Blakely. I can only say as to where H.J. Villipigue lived at that time that I understood where he lived by general report; I had never been there. I do not know where Charles Givens lived at that time, but I know where the Skinner place is. I understood Mr. Villipigue lived on that place. The Jule Skinner river place is a part of the A. Paulk place, it was known as the Skinner or Paulk place; it was

142

the Chattahoochee river place; in other words, the Coachman place. I understand it is the same place.

E.J. COACHMAN, sworn in behalf of the State, testified:

I knew H.J. Villipigue in his life time. He lived on my farm. That place was known first as the Paulk place, and then Jule Skinner bought it, and I bought it from Mr. Skinner. It is the Coachman place now. It was known as the Paulk place at first, and then Mr. Skinner bought it and it was known as the Skinner place, and I bought it from Skinner and I presume that it is now known as the Coachman place. It was known as the Skinner place down there. That is the place where H.J. Villipigue lived at the time he was killed. I know of no other place in Early county known as the Jules Skinner river place.

T.J. HOWELL, SR., sworn in behalf of the State, testified:

I am well acquainted in Early county. Have lived here fifty-three years. I am sheriff of the county and, as sheriff, am pretty familiar with Early county. There is not more than one place in Early county known as the Jules Skinner river place.

J.S. SHERMAN, recalled by the state, testified:

I stated that I knew where the Jules Skinner river place was located in this county. In going from Blakely to that place, the Skinner place, by my home is as direct a route as any you could take. I saw Granderson Goolsby on the day that Mr. Villipigue was killed, right after twelve o'clock, at my gate. He passed my gate in a buggy. It was a top buggy, the top was down; I cannot say whether it was a top or open buggy. I am pretty certain he was driving a mule. I cannot say that I remember the color of the mule. Granderson stopped there; two boys were with him. I did not notice the boys at all; Granderson rode by the gate with the two boys in the buggy, and I had no reason to pay any attention to them, except that I knew Granderson and he stopped beyond my gate about as far as from here to the door there. I did not notice the boys any more particularly; Granderson stopped the buggy just beyond my gate, got out of the buggy and came back to the gate where I was. When he stopped and came back, the boys in the buggy were in my view. There was nothing between where I was and the buggy where the boys were. It was in the day time. At that time, I made a casual look at the boys. I had occasion to look at them. One seemed to be darker than the other, a little shade darker. I cannot say as to their ages and sizes. They were seated in the buggy kinder with their backs to me. They were not grown, I don't think. Granderson Goolsby called my attention to them. Granderson Goolsby and I talked for twenty or thirty minutes. I don't think the conversation between Granderson Goolsby and I was in a tone loud enough to be heard by anybody in the buggy. He was talking very low to me and seemed to be cool and collected. Granderson Goolsby was going in the direction away from Blakely.

E.B. HAMILTON, sworn in behalf of the State, testified:
I live here in Blakely. I am in the hardware business. Have been in that business a little over four years. I knew H.J. Villipigue in his lifetime. I remember the day he was killed. I knew Granderson Goolsby. I don't know his two sons, Ulysses and Mike Goolsby. I saw Granderson Goolsby on the day it was said H.J. Villipigue was killed, in my store here in Blakely. It was between ten and eleven o'clock in the morning. At the time I saw him, there were two other parties with him; they were two negro boys. One appeared to be about fifteen or sixteen years old and the other about eighteen or twenty. Their complexion was black. After looking at those two parties there I cannot tell you whether or not there is any difference in the appearance of those boys who were with Granderson Goolsby on that occasion, the two boys there are practically of the same stature, but I cannot swear they are the same ones. I do not know of any difference between these two boys here and the two boys mentioned, but nearly all negroes of the same size and color look something alike.

CHARLES GIVENS, sworn in behalf of the state, testified:
I know the defendant in this case, Mike Goolsby. He is present in Court. The one sitting next to that white man there is Mike. That is him with the black pants on. I have been knowing the boy about three or four years. I have known Mike that long. I knew H. J. Villipigue. I remember the day he was killed. I know Ulysses Goolsby. He is present in Court; the one sitting next to you there. Granderson Goolsby was the father of Ulysses Goolsby and Mike Goolsby. I saw Mike Goolsby on the day Mr. Villipigue was killed, before he was killed. It was about one-thirty o'clock in the evening. Mike Goolsby and Ulysses Goolsby were in the buggy with their father, Granderson Goolsby. It was a top buggy, the top was down. They were driving a black mule. When I first saw them, they drove up in front of my house. I did not see them before they drove up there. When I first saw them, the mule and buggy had stopped in front of my house. The

road they were in ran east and west. It is about six miles from my house to Blakely. Mr. Villipigue lived at that time at the river, on Mr. Coachman's place. The road that leads to his house is the road that leads by my home. Mr. Villipigue lived about two miles from my house on that road, west from our house. Granderson Goolsby lived about three and a half or four miles north from where I lived. In going from Blakely to Granderson Goolsby's house in the most direct way, it would not be by my house; he would have to go a different road. In going from Granderson Goolsby's house to Mr. Villipigue's house, it would not be the most direct way for him to go to Blakely. I don't know exactly the most direct way from Granderson Goolsby's house to Blakely, as to distance; in my best judgment, it would be about five or six miles. In going the most direct route from Goolsby's house to my house, it would be about three and a half or four miles. If you went from Granderson Goolsby's house by Blakely and then go to my house, it would be close to about twelve miles; and then from my house to Mr. Villipigue's is about two miles. At the time I first saw Granderson Goolsby and Mike Goolsby and Ulysses Goolsby there in the road in front of the house, I was sitting down in the house, me and my father. It was about twelve yards from where I was sitting in the house to the road where the buggy stopped. No one got out of the buggy at my house. Granderson Goolsby said something, and at this time Mike and Ulysses Goolsby were sitting in the buggy with him. Granderson called for my father. They stopped and called my father and I got up and went to the door, and Granderson said, "Tell your father to step out here a minute", and I went and told my father and my father went out to the road where he was and he said he was going to see Mr. Villipigue; at this time Mike and Ulysses were sitting in the buggy; at this time while Granderson was doing the talking, my father was standing in the edge of the yard about three or four steps from the buggy. I was standing on the steps, about twelve yards away from the buggy. I heard what was said by Granderson Goolsby to my father; he said he wanted to see Mr. Villipigue; he said he understood he had whipped his boy, and he wanted to go and see if he couldn't give him some satisfaction about it. He asked my father if he could go and show him the way, and my father said no, that he did not feel like going and asked me if I would go and show him the way. All of the parties were present, and this defendant was present at the time. I told him I would go and show him the way. I rode a mule, and went with them. Nether Mike Goolsby or Ulysses Goolsby got out of the buggy at our house. That buggy remained standing until I caught my mule. The buggy and I moved off together. The buggy was in front. I was riding my mule. We went to Mr. Villipigue's house. We went directly there, and on the road straight down there. It took us about half an hour to get to Mr. Villipigue's house, going along at a moderate gait. We went through a gate across the road between my house and Mr. Villipigue house. The gate is about a quarter of a mile from Mr. Villipigue's house. The gate was shut and Mike Goolsby opened it. In opening the gate, Mike got out of the buggy. When they got to the gate, Ulysses and his father were on each side of the buggy seat and Mike Goolsby was sitting in the middle. The buggy had a dashboard, a board sitting up in front of the buggy. It was about a foot and a half, I reckon, from the rest of the buggy in which they were sitting to that dashboard, from the front edge of the seat. I know there was vacant space between the bottom of the buggy and the bottom of the top of the seat on which Granderson and his boys were sitting. I know there was vacant space in the back end of the buggy. It was near two feet, I guess from that seat, the front of the buggy on which they were sitting to the back part of the buggy. I could not tell whether, as Mike was sitting, his feet were on the bottom of the buggy or not. When he got to my house, his feet rested, it looked like on the bottom of the buggy. Mike got out of the buggy at the gate as we were going to Mr. Villipigue's, about a quarter of a mile from Mr. Villipigue's. Mike Goolsby got back in the buggy after he opened the gate, and he kept the same position he had been occupying before in the buggy. We went from there to Mr. Villipigue's house. His house faced south. The road continued on by Mr. Villipigue's house. It was a private road. When Granderson Goolsby and his two boys drove up in front of Mr. Villipigue's house, it placed Granderson Goolsby on the right side of the house, on the south side, as we drove up, the mule faced west; they stopped there. Granderson Goolsby spoke; when he spoke, he was in the buggy. Mike Goolsby at that time was in the buggy. Granderson Goolsby hailed and called Mr. Villipigue. I could not tell whether Mr. Villipigue answered or not. After Granderson called Mr. Villipigue, he was coming out of the house, and Granderson turned his buggy around. The mule was then facing east. They stopped when they faced the mule east. That throwed Ulysses Goolsby on the left, next to the house, and Granderson Goolsby was on the right, and Mike Goolsby was sitting in the middle. Mr. Villipigue was coming on out of the house, he was in his shirt sleeves; and I did not observe and weapon in Mr. Villipigue's hand or about him. I did not observe any weapon at all either in the possession of Ulysses Goolsby or Granderson Goolsby up to that time. Did not observe any weapon of any kind in the buggy they were in up to that time. As Mr. Villipigue was coming out, Granderson got out of the buggy on the south side; at this time, I did not see Mike Goolsby do anything. He changed his position in the buggy; he sat back in the place where his father was sitting Ulysses Goolsby did not change his position at all. After he got out of the buggy, Granderson Goolsby walked around on the side next to the house where Mr. Villipigue was. In going from the side of the buggy, he went around back of the buggy. He got as far as the front part of the hind wheel, the left hind wheel. That throwed Granderson Goolsby in hand's reach of Ulyesses Goolsby. At that time, Mike Goolsby was sitting by the side of Ulysses Goolsby in the buggy, on the same seat. There was a fence in front of Mr. Villipigue's home. There was a gate right out in front of the front door. There was a porch to the house that Mr. Villipigue lived in. There were steps leading up on the porch from the ground. The steps were directly north of the gate. It was about ten steps from the steps to the gate. The buggy was kinder southeast from the gate, about ten yards, I reckon. Mr. Villipigue came out of the gate. Mr. Villipigue did not say anything before he got out of the gate. He had gone about four or five steps from the gate before he, Mr. Villipigue, spoke. The first thing said by Mr. Villipigue was, he asked if that was the boy that he whipped that day. At the time Mr. Villipigue asked that, Granderson Goolsby was standing by his buggy, he had his hand resting on the left hind wheel. The top of the buggy was down. At that time, Granderson Goolsby said, "Yes, sir, this is my son". I will tell exactly what Mr. Villipigue said as near as I can remember it; Mr. Villipigue stopped and said, "Ain't that the boy I whipped yesterday". He was looking in the direction of Ulysses Goolsby at that time. Granderson Goolsby said, "Yes sir, that is my son; I brought him here to see if I could give you some satisfaction", and Mr. Villipigue said, "No; look out, I am going to kill him." Granderson turned and said, "No; you kill me first". Granderson turned back towards the buggy. He got his Winchester rifle from under the seat of the buggy; at this time Granderson was standing between the buggy wheels on the north side. I don't know exactly, sir, when he got the rifle out from under the seat of the buggy, which came out first, the stock or the barrel of the rifle. When Granderson Goolsby was getting his rifle, Mr. Villipigue fired his pistol. I don't know where the pistol came from; when I first saw it, it was in Mr. Villipigue's hand. Mr. Villipigue fired towards the buggy where they were-- Granderson Goolsby and Ulysses and Mike Goolsby. Mr. Villipigue fired the pistol three times to my best recollection, once while Granderson was getting his rifle. Granderson grabbed his rifle out from under the seat of the buggy and ran backwards towards the river, kinder south; he walked back about three or four steps; up to that time, Mr. Villipigue had fired once. Granderson Goolsby fired the next shot. The next shot was fired by Mr. Villipigue with his pistol, he turned then and shot towards Granderson Goolsby the second shot. Granderson Goolsby fired the next shot with a rifle towards Mr. Villipigue. The next shot was fired by Mr. Villipigue. Mr. Villipigue shot three times. Granderson Goolsby fired next with a rifle. Mr. Villipigue, at this time, the last shot fired by Granderson Goolsby that I have described, dropped his right hand down by his side. Villipigue had his pistol in his right hand; his right hand dropped down by his side. He turned and started back towards the house in the direction of the gate. He went into the gate. When Mr. Villipigue got to the gate, Ulysses fired at him with a breechloader. I cannot exactly say, it was before Mr. Villipigue got to the gate, or just after he passed through the gate, but as near as I could say he was entering the gate when Ulysses fired; while entering the gate, Mr. Villipigue was facing his house; that made his face north. Ulysses fired with a double-barrel breech loaded shot gun. He got the gun out from under the seat of the buggy. That was the same place from where Granderson Goolsby got his rifle. At that particular time when Ulysses Goolsby got the shot gun from under the seat of the buggy, like Goolsby was sitting in the buggy. Mike Goolsby had the lines, I think, I am not sure he did. The length of the gun Ulysses got out from under the seat of the buggy and shot was near three feet. The rifle that Granderson Goolsby got out from the seat of the buggy was near the same length. The reason I had not seen the rifle and shot gun, there was a croker sack over them. I had seen the croker sack. No, sir, I paid no attention to it, and had not seen the croker sack before we got to Mr. Villipigue's house. The croker sack was spread over the stocks of the guns. The stocks of the guns were in the front part of the buggy. When Ulysses Goolsby got the gun from under the seat, he was sitting in the buggy. He then jumped out of the buggy and shot. He walked about three steps from the buggy and shot. He walked towards Mr. Villipigue. He stopped when he was firing the gun. He fired the gun in the direction of Mr. Villipigue. I cannot exactly tell whether or not Mr. Villipigue had his back, side or face towards Ulysses Goolsby when he fired the gun, but he was entering the gate. He was going from Ulysses Goolsby. At the time Ulysses Goolsby fired the shot gun, as I have described, he was about ten or twelve steps from Mr. Villipigue. The buggy was facing the east, and Mike Goolsby and Ulysses Goolsby were sitting in the buggy facing east, and they were in that position when Mr.

Villipigue's arm dropped to his side. At the time Mr. Villipigue's arm dropped to his side, he was standing at the side of the buggy, a little, kinder front of the buggy. Ulysses Goolsby is a little bigger than Mike Goolsby. Ulysses Goolsby weighs about 130 or 140 pounds, and Mike weighs about the same. At the time Mr. Villipigue was killed, Mike Goolsby seemed to be the smaller; I cannot tell you how many pounds smaller was Mike Goolsby at that time than Ulysses Goolsby—about ten pounds difference then, is the best I could say. I do not know exactly how many times Ulysses Goolsby fired the shotgun in the direction of Mr. Villipigue; in my best judgment, once or twice. Mr. Villipigue kept walking when Ulysses fired the gun. He walked in the same direction when the gun was fired and after the gun was fired. After Ulysses Goolsby fired the shot gun, Granderson Goolsby fired the Winchester rifle. At this time, he was standing by the buggy. Granderson Goolsby had moved from the position from which he had fired last before that at Mr. Villipigue back towards the buggy two or three steps; that put him no closer and no further to Mr. Villipigue, but kinder on the side of him. That put him more directly in front of Mr. Villipigue's front door. It put him more in front of the front door when shooting at Mr. Villipigue at the last. When Granderson Goolsby stepped up towards the buggy, as I said, and fired the last shot, as I have described, Mr. Villipigue was going towards the house. At that time Mr. Villipigue was about half way between the gate and the steps. After that no other shots were fired. That was the last shot fired. I cannot tell whether Mr. Villipigue stopped when the last shot was fired. I turned and walked off when the last shot was fired. Mr. Villipigue had not fallen at the time I turned; when I saw him he was going towards the steps. I afterwards looked up towards the house. I saw Mr. Villipigue then. I could see the front of the house I could see the porch. I did not see Mr. Villipigue. I did not see Mr. Villipigue's wife. I do not know what became of the pistol Mr. Villipigue had in his hand when his arm dropped down to his side. I did not see the pistol any more after that. I am no kin to this defendant, Mike Goolsby and I am no kin to Granderson Goolsby and Ulysses Goolsby. I never did work for Mr. Villipigue. After these shots were fired, Granderson Goolsby and Ulysses got in the buggy and they and Mike started off. When Granderson and Ulysses Goolsby got in the buggy, Mike was in the buggy. That was the same buggy they went out there in. They started back east. After they had gone about thirty yards they stopped. When they stopped, Granderson Goolsby got out. I don't know exactly which one of them was driving the mule then. I know that Ulysses Goolsby and Granderson Goolsby, after they quit shooting, placed the rifle and shot gun in the same position where they were, under the seat of the buggy. I did not pay any attention as to which one of them put both guns back under the seat of the buggy; I don't know, sir, but they put them back. All three, after Granderson and Ulysses got back in the buggy, drove off about thirty yards and stopped. Granderson got out of the buggy and went back in front of the gate and picked up his croker sack, the croker sack what the guns were wrapped up in. I do not exactly know when, the croker sack fell out of the buggy, but to my best recollection when Granderson Goolsby got his rifle out of the buggy. After Granderson Goolsby got his croker sack, he turned and went back to the buggy and they all went on towards home. They went on back home; they were in the buggy together; Granderson, Ulysses and Mike Goolsby. When I last saw them they were going towards their home. When I last saw them they passed my house. I saw them for about fifty yards after they passed my home, Granderson, Ulysses and Wike Goolaby were in the buggy going towards their home when I last saw them.

--Cross Examined:--

I heard the conversation between my father and Granderson Goolsby at my father's house. My purpose in going along with them was because I was asked to go and show them the way. I did not expect any trouble up there. Everything appeared peaceful, that is the Goolsbys were not doing anything to show a hostile act. When we got up to Mr. Villipigue's house, and when Granderson Goolsby called him out, he said, "Hello, Mr. Henry". The tone in which he spoke was not a loud or angry tone. It was a peaceful tone. Mr. Villipigue got up as soon as Granderson called him and come walking out of the house. He come directly on out of the gate. He did not stop, came towards the buggy then. Mr. Villipigue spoke first. He asked if that want the boy he whipped yesterday. He was pointing towards Ulysses Goolsby. Granderson Goolsby then said, "Yes, sir; that is my son; I come to see if I can give you some satisfaction." Mr. Villipigue then said, "No, look out, I am going to kill him." When he said that, Granderson Goolsby turned to get his rifle. When Mr. Villipigue said "I am going to kill him", he did not draw his pistol right then; I did not see him make any motion. When I knowed anything, he had his pistol in his hand Mr. Villipigue pointed his pistol when Granderson Goolsby was getting his rifle. When Mr. Villipigue said that, Granderson Goolsby turned around towards the buggy. When Granderson turned around with his gun, he shot at him. At that time, Granderson Goolsby had not shot his gun; Granderson Goolsby was standing then between the wheels of the buggy getting his gun. When the shooting started, it was pretty fast and pretty rapid. All of the shotting occurred along pretty fast. At this time, I jumped off of the mule and got out of the way. I was looking back all the while. I looked in front of me. The mule that they were driving, not that I know of was trying to run off. I did not see the mule trying to run. He was making no effort to get away. My mule was. I got off of my mule while the shooting was going on. Mike Goolsby was holding the mule hitched to the buggy. I did not see him doing nothing. I was looking back. If Mike had anything, I could have seen him. I did not try to get out of the way. I did not see Mike doing anything more then I did. I had a good opportunity to see what they done. I did not see anybody else there. I did not hear Mr. Villipigue, while the shotting was going on, holler for some one to bring his gun. He called his wife, I know he hollered for his wife, that is all I understood him to say,--called his wife. He might have said "Bring me my gun", but I did not understand that. Mr. Villipigue said something. He said something while the shooting was going on. He hollered and said something to his wife, and started back to his house and called his wife. I don't know what he said. When we all went back from there, I went on back home. I told my father about what I had seen up there at Mr. Villipigue's house. I have been in this county all my life. I have been farming. I have been doing nothing for the last six months, I have been in jail. I was put in there on this case. I do not know that I have been indicted for any charge. I have not been notified of any indictment for any charge. I have talked to no one about this case. I have told the sheriff how it was, and Mr. Castellow, too, and I went before the Grand Jury.

MRS. IRENE VILLIPIGUE, sworn for the State, testified:

H.J. Villipigue was my husband. I was living with him at the time of his death. He is now dead. He was killed, in Early county, on December 29, 1915. He was shot. My husband and I were living at the time he was shot on Mr. E.H. Coachman's farm, located in the western part of Early county, near the Chattahoochee river. There is a road in front of the premises. Just before my husband was killed, I had been to Griffin, Ga. I came home the day he was killed. My husband took me home in the buggy from Blakely. We reached home about 12:30 o'clock in the afternoon. Just before my husband was killed, I was asleep, in the room on the west side of the house. I do not know when my husband left the room; I was asleep at the time. The shooting in front of the house waked me up. I could not tell whether it sounded like a rifle or pistol shot. When I woke up and heard the shooting, my husband called me to carry him the shot gun. I got up off the bed, took the shot gun, and went to the front door. That door led into the hall. I did not go any further than the front hall door. From the front hall door there was nothing to obstruct my view from the front of the house. When I got to the hall door, I saw three negroes and my husband. Two of the negroes were shooting at my husband. At the time these two negroes were shooting at him, he was coming towards the house. At this time he was just on the outside of the gate. He continued on coming towards the house. He opened the gate. I do not know what the negroes were doing while he was opening the gate. I was looking at him. When my husband opened the gate, he came on towards the house. He did not stop between the gate and the house. He did not stop at all from the time I saw him coming towards the house until he got to the house. Two of them were shooting. They were shooting with a pistol and gun. Each one had a pistol and a gun, the two that were doing the shooting. The third one was sitting in the buggy holding the mule. The buggy was as far from where the two negroes were doing the shooting as far as from me to the wall. My husband came into the house; he came in by the front door. I was standing by the side of the door when he came in. He fell against me; after that he lived just a few minutes. When he died, he was lying in the hall. I did not know either one of the three negroes I saw in front of the house, and I did not know the names of either one of them. I can look at these two negroes sitting here and say that one of those two was there, the one sitting on the right. The one next to you. He was shooting. I do not know that the other one was there. I could not identify the one sitting in the buggy; I could just see one arm of him. The things I have stated occurred in this county on the 29th of December, 1915. The first person that got there after my husband was killed was several negroes and one white man, who came up about the same time. The white man was Mr. McCullough. After the shooting, I saw the negroes going off down the road. Two of them were walking behind the buggy and want in it the last I saw of them. They stopped and the two out of the buggy turned and come back towards the house and turned and went back. I do not know what they came back for.

--Cross-Examined:--

When I heard the shooting, I was asleep in the bed in my room. The shooting waked me up. The shots were fired kinder rapidly. All of the shots come kinder along together. I heard my husband call me to bring his gun. When he called for his gun, it was during the shooting. I got the gun and started to the door, I got to the front door. I saw three negroes out there. I did not see the fourth one. I did not see the one riding the mule. I only saw one mule, the one hitched to the buggy. I saw one in the buggy holding the reins. I do not remember how the person in the buggy held the reins. I just saw him in the buggy.

--Examined Redirect:--

I did not see my husband with any weapon of any kind in his hand when I got to the front door and saw him. I did not see any weapon in his hand at all during the progress of the difficulty. When the last shot was fired by the negroes, my husband was lying in the hall. The last shot was fired with a pistol. The bullet struck the front screen door; that was the same door my husband had gone through. The same ones were shooting with pistols who had been shooting with guns before that.

M.M. MCCULLOUGH, sworn in behalf of the State, testified:

I knew H.J. Villipigue in his lifetime. On the day he was killed, I was on the place near the house hauling some wood for him. I saw four negroes come to the house before he was killed. Three in a buggy driving a black mule, and one riding a sorrel mule. I couldn't recognize any of the individuals, but I thought I did recognize the black mule, but I want sure about that. I was too far off to recognize the four men; I was about three hundred yards west and there was nothing to prevent me seeing them except the wire fence between us. At that time, I was going back after a load of wood, and I was hauling wood right up west to the stockade, and I had just left the stockade. I cannot say that I heard shooting back up at the house after I left; I thought I did and stopped the wagon, but there was no other report made, but there was a loose blank on the carry-log on the wagon and it made some fuss as the wagon went along, kinder of a rattling noise. I heard something after that about Mr. Villipigue having been shot. After I stopped my wagon, it was between three, five and eight minutes that I thought I heard some shooting. A negro boy came to me and told me about Mr. Villipigue having been shot. I then went to the house where Mr. Villipigue was. It was his home. I went into the hall where he was lying dead, and picked him up and put him on the bed. There was a negro man in there that lived on the place; he went in just ahead of me; he walked in just ahead of me. I found Mr. Villipigue dead; he was lying in the hall, right up in the northeast corner of the hall; his house sits east and west. and he was in the northeast corner of the hall. I observed one wound on him, in his right side. I did not make any close examination. I saw no weapon about his body or person. I did not see any weapon of any kind in the yard as I went in, but after I picked him up and put him on the bed, I walked back out in the yard and found a pistol lying about eight feet from the yard gate, in the yard, between the gate and the steps. I had seen this pistol. I know whose pistol it was; it was Mr. Villipigue's pistol. I did examine it; I have forgot whether there were two or three cartridges in it which had been shot out. It was a pistol that shot six times, and two or three had been shot, and the rest in it were loaded cartridges. There was no sign of any of the other cartridges in the pistol which were loaded having been snapped on at all; that was all the weapon I found there. I saw the four negroes when they left. The last I saw of them, the mule run off with the one in the buggy and he stopped the mule up about the wire fence and the others come and got in it. Three come and got in it. I am not related to H.J. Villipigue.

J.O. BRIDGES, sworn in behalf of the State, testified:

I knew H.J. Villipigue in his lifetime. I saw his dead body the same day he was killed. I think it was just a little after dark. I know it on the same day he was killed. When I first saw his body, it was at his home on a bed. I helped prepare his body for burial, and I saw his body after his clothes were removed from him. I noticed wounds upon his body. There was a wound on his right arm, a bullet wound, and the ball entered just below the elbow, in front just below the elbow, about here, and lodged under the skin just above the elbow, and there was a bullet wound in the back of his head, just to the right of the center of his head, and went through and lodged over his left eye. That bullet entered to the right of the center of the back of his head and lodged over his left eye; it did not come through; you could feel the ball a little bit over his left eye, and there was another wound that sniffed his right ear, and went into the temple about here. It went in the temple just in front of the ear, and there were various wounds in other places on his body. All of the wounds were located in the rear or back of his body, except the one in the right arm. The wounds on his back appeared to be wounds made by a gun loaded with buckshot, except the one that went under the right shoulder blade and come diagonally and lodged at his left nipple and bulged the skin up; it bulged out the left nipple above and below, I would judge it bulged out a place four inches in diameter. The wound that entered under the right shoulder from the rear was about the size of my thumb; my thumb could enter the hole all right. There were other bullets and shot picked out of his back; they were buckshot In the back between the shoulders and down about his hips. I do not remember exactly how many were picked out; two or three picked out just under the skin. I had had experience with firearms, and to observe the effect of shot fired from guns or weapons in the nature of fire arms; I have had experience as to the effect of wounds made on the human body which had been made by fire arms. I have had experience with a cut shell, and have shot cut shells. A cut shell is an ordinary shot gun shell loaded up and a knife taken and cut around the shell where the wadding separates the powder from the shell and when the shell is exploded, the whole end of the shell where it is cut around blows off and carries the shot in a wad. The front part of the shell. From my observation of that wound I have described just under the right shoulder of Mr. Villipigue's body, and from my knowledge of fire arms and the use of them, I would say that it was inflicted from a cut shell fired from a shot gun. The range of a cut shell shot from a shot gun, would shoot further; it would hold the shot together a longer distance, and hit a body in a wad, and would not scatter the shot like an ordinary shell shot from the same gun at the same distance. From my observation as to how that wound entered the body, the direction of it, and my observation of the bulge out about the left nipple, I would say it was caused by the shot that entered the wound under the right shoulder and came through the body and bulged the skin out at the left nipple without going through. I am not kin to Mr. H.J. Villipigue in any way. The wound I spoke of in the right arm showed that the right arm was broken just below the elbow.

M. COHEN, sworn in behalf of the State, testified:
I knew H.J. Villipigue in his lifetime; I saw his body after his death; I helped to prepare his body for burial; I saw his body after the clothing had been removed. I observed wounds on his body. There was a wound right below the elbow, on the right arm, the bullet entering from just below the elbow; the bullet did not come out; it lodged back around behind the elbow, above his elbow; we could feel it.

And there was a wound in the back under the right shoulderblade. It was the biggest wound he had. It was big enough for you to get your thumb in. I saw other wounds on his body; on the back of his body, it was badly peppered up, and it looked like it might have been made with buckshot. There was a wound that grazed the ear and went into the temple; there was a wound on the back of his head. It entered right near the center of the back of his head. It did not come through. I did not see any evidences of its coming through. I am not kin to Mr. Villipigue in any way.

DR. C.R. BARKSDALE, sworn in behalf of the State, testified:

My profession is the practice of medicine. I have practiced medicine sixteen years continuously. I knew H. . Villipigue in his lifetime and I saw his body after he was dead. I found wounds on his body, there was one in the forearm, just below the in elbow, which broke both bones the right forearm, and the bullet ranged up and lodged just above the elbow; both bones were broken in the arm below the elbow. That bullet lodged back of the elbow, about the elbow joint; you could feel it. I found other wounds on him; there was one in the back under the right shoulder blade; that hole was big enough to put my thumb in, and appeared to have been made with a load of shot. That wound, or that load rather, did not come through his body. Did not see other wounds, only some scattered shots. From my observation of the wounds I saw on the person of H.J. Villipigue after his death, my opinion is that the round in the back under the right shoulder blade caused his death. This was the biggest wound I observed. The wound in the arm that I have described was not necessarily a fatal wound. I did not examine Mr. Villipigue's head. I am no kin to Mr. Villipigue in any way.

T.J. HOWELL, SR., sworn in behalf of the State, testified:

I am sheriff of this county. I remember when H.J. Villipigue was killed. I knew Granderson Goolsby. I know Mike and Ulysses Goolsby. After the death of Mr. Villipigue, I made every effort to find the defendant, Mike Goolsby. I did everything possible to find him in Early county. I had assistance in the matter. I could not locate him and Early county. I did finally find him after the death of Mr. Villipigue. I cannot be positive as to how long, but about four weeks. I found the defendant, Mike Goolsby, in the state of Mississippi. Don't know exactly how far from Blakely. I went to Mississippi after him. After the death of Mr. Villipigue,

I do not know the name of the little town just now where I first saw Mike Goolsby. It was in the Delta belt, the Mississippi valley, in the western part of Mississippi, near the Mississippi River; my best recollection, it was about 700 miles, I think; I used up about 700 miles of mileage script. This was not on the round-trip, on the straight trip, the way I traveled. Ulysses Goolsby, a brother of Mike Goolsby, and son of Granderson Goolsby, was with Mike at the time. They were together when I first saw them in Mississippi after the death of Mr. Villipigue. I went there for the purpose of bringing them back to Early County. I did not bring them to Early County; I carried them to Fulton County. I had a warrant for their arrest.

(Evidence for the State here closed.)

--STATEMENT OF THE DEFENDANT:--

Please, your Honor, Solicitor General, and gentlemen of the jury: I am before you this evening to make a statement. On the day this occurred, early that morning, when I come home, I learned of this trouble, and when I got home, my father said that we had to go with him over there, me and my brother, and see Mr. Villipigue so he could have a talk with Mr. Villipigue. I did not want to go, me and my brother, but he had to force us to get in the buggy and go. So we come on to town here that morning, and while we were here in town, my father talked to some men here in town, but he would leave us sitting in the buggy, and I don't know what he was talking about. We left town here, and my father drove on out until we got to Charlie Givens' father's house, and he wont there, and my father goes on up to Charlie Givens' house. When he got to Charlie Givens house, he called and Charlie Givens come to the door, and asked him where his father was, and his father come to the door, and he asked him to go with him down to Mr. Villipigue's to show him the way, and Mr. Givens was sick, so he said, and did not desire to go. Therefore, Mr. Givens asked his son, Charlie Givens, to go and show my father the way down to Mr. Villipigue's, and Charlie Givens went and got his mule and come on out in the road, and we went on down to Mr. Villipigue's house. When we got to Mr. Villipigue's house, my father called Mr. Villipigue and said "Mr. Henry", and Mr. Henry come to the door, and when Mr. Henry come to the door, he walked on out of the gate and walked about five steps from the gate, not very far from the buggy, and he stopped and looked towards the buggy, and at that time he said, "Ain't that the boy I whipped yesterday", and my father said, "Yes, this is my son", and Mr. Villipigue asked if he had come to take it up, and my father said, "No, sir", that he had just come to talk it over with him, and Mr. Villipigue said, "Get out of the way, I am going to kill him", and my father said, "No, sir, don't kill him, kill me". And at that time, Mr. Villipigue begin to shoot, and the mule got frightened, and my father reached and got his gun and him and Mr. Villipigue were shooting at each other, and I cannot say how many shots were made, but I know at the time the shooting took place, the mule got nervous and broke to run and that left me and my brother in the buggy, and the mule run about twenty steps before I got the mule stopped. Before I got the mule stopped, the shooting was going on, and I couldn't see behind me what was going on, because I was holding the mule. Soon after I got the mule stopped, my father come on back the way the mule run and get in the buggy and we come on home. I did not know that my father was going up there to harm anybody no more than by what he said; he said he wont going up there to harm anybody, but said he was just going up there to talk it over with Mr. Villipigue. I was not going up there to harm anybody. And I had nothing to do with it, only my father made me go along with him up there. Therefore, we come on home, and my father sent us off to keep from getting hurt; he sent us off, and that is why we left home, and not for any crime that we had done. When I went up there with my father, I did not know any trouble was going to happen, and, therefore, I am here, and I make my statement to you to the best of my regard, and that is all I know. At the time that occurred, I was only fifteen years old, but in this year, in the month of July, on the 13th, I was sixteen years old, but at that time I was only fifteen, making me sixteen now, going on seventeen at present.

(The evidence in the case here closed on both sides.)

ABOUT THE AUTHOR

Photograph by Edward LaRose.

T he career highlights of Orice Jenkins have covered more ground than he ever could've imagined as a singer-songwriter, genealogy researcher and executive director of a nonprofit organization. His journey as an author started with unearthing the stories of formerly enslaved Americans on his blog, *Chesta's Children*. Since then, Orice's work has been featured in the *Washington Post*, UsefulCharts.com, Finding Your Roots and on the National Park Service website. He is a member of the Afro-American Historical and Genealogical Society; the American Society of Composers, Authors and Publishers; and a charter member of the Sons and Daughters of the United States Middle Passage.

Visit his website: oricejenkins.com.

Visit us at
www.historypress.com